'81

Tom
Christmas

Still hoping

FOR FATHERS WHO AREN'T IN HEAVEN

·RON RAND·

Regal Books
A Division of GL Publications
Ventura, California, U.S.A.

Published by Regal Books
A Division of GL Publications
Ventura, California 93006
Printed in U.S.A.

Library of Congress Cataloging-in-Publication Data

Rand, Ron, 1942-
   For fathers who aren't in heaven.

   Bibliography: p.
   1. Family—Religious life.   I. Title.
BV4526.2.R355   1986   248.8′421   86-27979
ISBN 0-8307-1214-3

2 3 4 5 6 7 8 9 10 / 91 90 89 88 87

Rights for publishing this book in other languages are contracted by Gospel Literature International (GLINT) foundation. GLINT also provides technical help for the adaptation, translation, and publishing of Bible study resources and books in scores of languages worldwide. For further information, contact GLINT, Post Office Box 488, Rosemead, California, 91770, U.S.A., or the publisher.

Dedication

To Louis and Josie for the family memories they have provided as grandparents.

To Charles and Ruth for the family modeling they have provided as parents.

To Jennifer, Josh, Nate and Chris for the motivation and joy they are providing as family members.

To John Bollinger and the men in the FATHERS Ministry at College Hill Presbyterian Church for the family mainstay they have provided as partners in ministry.

To David Freas and Star Luteri-Hicks for the title and manuscript they have provided as contributors to this book.

Contents

1

A Very Successful Failure

"I'm deeply concerned about the failure of our past to equip us to be
effective husbands and fathers."

7

2

Getting to Know the Lord, Others and You!

"There are multiple differences among individuals that have nothing to do
with right and wrong, good or bad."

23

3

How to Share Your Schedules

"Sharing your schedules can be God's way of giving you peace at all
times."

41

4

What About Your Children's Mom?

"The most important someone else is your wife."

55

5

Taking Time to Be with Your Family

"Schedule appointments with your family members? There are no clients
more important or deserving of your time."

75

6

Inventive Family Worship

"It just doesn't work when we say, 'Com'on you kids, sit down and shut up. We're gonna worship now!'"

95

7

Giving Thanks and Encouragement

"It's more difficult to think of someone who does not need appreciation and encouragement."

117

8

Creating Family Fun Times

"May our children not look back on a void, recalling only their own individual conquests."

135

9

Spicing Up Your Sex Life

"Sex is not a spiritual gift. It's a learned behavior that can become a beautiful expression when learned well."

155

10

Leading Your Children to Christ

"Most kids are expected to 'get religion' by osmosis. Let's pass on the good news ourselves!"

177

Appendix
207

Notes
217

Bibliography
221

Chapter 1

A Very Successful Failure

All we like sheep have gone astray; we have turned, every one, to his own way; and the LORD has laid on Him the iniquity of us all (Isa. 53:6, NKJV).

Monday night was hot and muggy, and it was long past nine o'clock, when the program was supposed to have been over. Too many people were crowded into the fellowship hall. I was sweaty and uncomfortable, but it was apparent that no one was willing to cut the session short. Every eye was glued to the overhead screen.

We were watching Dr. James Dobson's *Focus on the Family* film series; specifically, the film on Christian fathering. At a certain point in the film, Dr. Dobson asked the men to stand and make a prayer of recommitment to be better husbands and fathers. I think every man in the room stood up, including me. When the film was finished and the lights came on, I could see tears in many eyes.

There was a lot of hugging and several small groups gathered in different corners for more prayer.

As I walked the last couples to the parking lot, we were full of enthusiasm—we were going to be more sensitive to our spouses, we would spend more time with our kids and we would stop the fussing and whining in our families. Powered by the Holy Spirit, we would build the kind of Christian homes that Dr. Dobson had described. We could do it!

Six weeks later, I found myself coming home from still another late-night meeting. The house was quiet, Jennifer was already in bed and the boys had been prayed with and tucked in long ago. I sat down on the steps in the dark and thought about that recommitment I had made after the Dobson film. Had anything changed in six weeks?

Had I been more sensitive to Jennifer's needs? I thought back to that afternoon when Jennifer had been trying to talk to me while I worked on the checkbook. Sure, she knew that I could do two things at once. But was I fulfilling her need for my attention?

What about my kids? How was I reflecting the heavenly Father to Joshua, Nathan and Christopher? I had promised Joshua I would practice baseball with him and after six weeks of promises, the bat, ball and glove were all still in the locker.

I had promised Nathan that I would fix the chain and seat on his bicycle. But my schedule had taken me out of town, so his mother had tried her best to adjust the bike while I was gone. Now the seat was wobbling and the chain was slipping again.

I had promised Chris that we would work together on his model train, to lay more track and finish some more inclines. During all these weeks, we hadn't touched it.

When was the last time I had tucked the boys into bed?

Last night? No, I had been at a committee meeting at church. Two nights ago? No, I had been with the evangelism team and the evening before that I had watched the game on TV. Last week? Yes, on Thursday I had taken the boys upstairs and read them a story, but they had complained that they wanted their mommy to tuck them into bed instead of me!

As I sat on the steps in the dark, my coat halfway off and a crumpled outline of the meeting's agenda in my hand, it was obvious that my boys had a father who was busy, distracted and absent most of the time. Other people's needs, the church's needs, the committees' needs and everything else seemed more urgent than being a daddy.

Oh, I was busy with important things. I co-pastored a church with well over 2,000 active members, held evangelism clinics across the nation and overseas plus performed "regular" pastoral duties. I was plenty busy. Life was controlled by the little black appointment book of the "successful" executive. I had indeed tasted a measure of success, but tonight, sitting alone on the stairway in the dark, I realized that I was *very* successful—abundantly, overwhelmingly successful at being a failure as a father!

What Went Wrong?

What happened to my good intentions? I really wanted to be a good father. My commitment had been so sincere. I had been so inspired! But that inspiration had been like a fourth of July sparkler—it burned brightly for a while then faded. Six weeks later nothing had changed, except that I had made more promises and broken every one. I was thoroughly disgusted with myself. The answer was not to read another book, take another class or listen to more tapes. I was tired of being inspired! I needed a way to turn inspiration into action!

In the next few days I made a point of looking up other fathers who had attended the Dobson series. I asked if they had seen any change in their homes. Again and again the answer was the same: "Ron, I've tried to change, but, well, I just can't stick to it."

I talked to at least 14 fathers and didn't find one who was able to identify a concrete change in his life!

Before going any further, I want to say that the problem isn't with Dr. Dobson's film series or with the principles he teaches. I am deeply grateful to James Dobson because his material was the means that God used to demonstrate just how deep was the need to change our habits.

The problem is *change*. I want to be able to make a decision, stick to it, and then 6 or 8 or 10 weeks later, look back and say, "Yes, indeed, I can see a difference in my life!" In order to do this we need specifics. Exactly what needs to be changed? Let's look at three specific areas where I see the greatest need and the greatest possibility of change.

Time with the Father

> Blessed is the man . . . his delight is in the law
> of the LORD, and on his law he meditates day
> and night. He is like a tree planted by streams
> of water . . . . In all that he does, he prospers
> (Ps. 1:1-3).

How much time do you spend talking and listening to God each day? If you are like myself and the men I interviewed, the answer is probably, "Not very much." And yet we call ourselves Christians, disciples of Jesus Christ.

What does that word "disciple" mean? It means, "disciplined one." If we are to become effective fathers, it seems to me that our first need is to become disciplined in our devotional lives.

Looking in Scripture, we find many examples of men who made time with God their first priority. There is Moses, who perhaps spent more time with God than any other man in the Old Testament. Exodus 33:11 testifies, "The Lord used to speak to Moses face to face, as a man speaks to his friend." Then there is Jesus Himself, in the New Testament: "In these days he went out into the hills to pray; and all night he continued in prayer to God" (Luke 6:12). If it was important for Moses and Jesus to make time to pray (and think how busy they were!), surely we can find a few minutes in each day to be with the Father of fathers.

Now, please don't misunderstand me. I'm not talking about the problem of *how* to go about having time alone with God. There are plenty of study guides, prayer manuals, and other resources available. I am talking about the problem of having enough self-discipline to sit down and *do it*; namely regular, consistent and faithful time with God. This is where I find most men stumbling and experiencing the most guilt. This is the first area where we need a plan to help us achieve the vision.

Husbands, Love Your Wives and Children

Husbands, love your wives, as Christ loved the church and gave himself up for her (Eph. 5:25).

Fathers, do not provoke your children to anger, but bring them up in the discipline and instruction of the Lord (Eph. 6:4).

The second need I see among Christian men is to learn *how* to love their wives and children. Most husbands want to love their spouses and try so hard to do so. But too many husbands feel like failures: "I know I should spend more time with her," we say, "but somehow I get so busy." Or, "I want to tell her I love her, but I just don't know how to say it right." Or, "We used to do so many things together, but now with the kids and both of us working, we don't ever seem to see each other." Men don't automatically know how to love their wives and children; we need to be taught. How many church curricula include such a course in their educational programs? Ours didn't. Why not?

Fences and Families

Not long ago I built a fence in our yard and I learned a few things about both fences and families. One third of the height of a fence has to be in the ground for the fence to stand strong against stress. You don't see that part, but it is the foundation that holds the fence together. Christian marriage is like that; one third of the marriage—the invisible strong foundation—is Jesus Christ.

The wood that I used to build the fence has been treated to resist the mildew and the rot and termites. Christian families have the Holy Spirit, creating faithfulness and humility in each member and protecting us against mildew, rot of the spirit and the bugs that eat their way in to destroy relationships.

The salesperson who sold me the fence posts said that all the wood is protected, except for the knots. The termites can eat the knots. Satan would like to find the "knots" in our lives—the grudges, the little irritations—

and rip apart our families. We need to be continually filled with the Holy Spirit.

I used a level to check how each fence post was set. At times I put the level on one side, and from my point of view, it seemed level. But from another perspective, that same pole was sometimes completely off. I needed to go around to the other side and see that the pole was level from that angle as well.

Many times in my family interractions I need to get Jennifer's point of view and each child's point of view so we can "level" with one another.

So the first need is to put God first in our lives, to become disciplined disciples. The second need is to learn *how* to love our wives and children: to build a foundation for our marriages in Jesus Christ, to learn about the unique qualities of the members of our families and to learn to communicate and share our feelings. But more than just recognizing our needs, I wanted to find a method by which men could support and encourage and hold each other accountable to really *do* what we had been inspired to do.

That brings us to what I see as our third greatest need.

Redeem the Time

Look carefully then how you walk, not as unwise men but as wise, making the most of the time, because the days are evil (Eph. 5:15-16).

The third greatest need among Christian men is to learn how to make the most of the time; how to spend individual and personal time with each family member. Both qualitative and quantitative times are needed. It's difficult to have a qualitative time without having quantitative time. The quantity of time leads to the quality of time in most cases. Again Dr. Dobson hit home in my heart and head when he wrote:

> I have already admitted that I have also struggled to achieve a proper perspective between my profession and my family. Just when I think I have conquered the dragon of overcommitment, I say "yes" a few times when I should have said, "no, thanks," and the monster arises to maul me again. I know of no easier mistake to make, nor one that has such devastating implications for the family.
>
> Nevertheless, the worst siege of overcommitment I've ever experienced came in the fall of 1977. I went through six weeks of incredible pressure, involving obligations that should have been spread over six months. I still don't know what wave of stupidity caused me to yield to such nonsense. I wasn't forced. No one threatened my life. I was not financially pressed. I can recall having no excuse. I simply relaxed my guard for a few weeks and found myself in a race for survival . . . . The climax occurred in early October when I flew to Cincinnati to participate in a Praise Gathering, sponsored by Mr. Bill Gaither.[1]

When I read that passage I felt like I'd been shot with a double-barreled guilt gun! First of all, my own College Hill Presbyterian Church was instrumental in bringing Dobson to that Cincinnati Praise Gathering. Secondly, if Dobson struggled with overcommitment, what hope was left for the rest of us?

Fifteen Wonderful Seconds

Back in the '70s, some researchers wanted to find out how much time fathers spent playing and talking with their children. In interviews, fathers estimated that they spent 15-20 seconds a day with each of their kids. The researchers decided to check that out. They devised a way to attach little microphones to toddlers' T-shirts and actually listened in on the conversations that went on in the homes. They were horrified with the results. "The average amount of time spent by these middle-class fathers with their small children was thirty-seven seconds per day! Their direct interaction was limited to 2.7 encounters daily, lasting ten to fifteen seconds each!"[2]

The average American child spends somewhere between six to seven hours a day, 30 to 50 hours a week, watching TV. Where are our children learning their values—from the concern of their parents or the commercials on television? Who is their strongest role model—Dad or the Dukes? When the kids get off the school bus, do they run to tell Dad what's been going on in their day or do they run to turn on the tube? Once again, although we may be convinced that we *need* to spend time with our families, without some method to hold one another accountable, there is little possibility of success.

The apostle Paul admonishes, "Look carefully then how you walk, not as unwise [people] but as wise, making the most of the time, because the days are evil" (Eph. 5:15-16). There are two words in the Greek language that Paul might have chosen in the phrase "making the most of the time": *chronos* and *kairos,* both translated by the English word, "time." *Chronos* has the sense of a general age, an eon, or the Greek philosophers' concept of the unending stream of time. The other word, *kairos,* indi-

15

cates a specific time that will not happen again—an opportunity to be seized because it won't be offered again. As I studied this passage, it seemed the Holy Spirit was saying that I am only going to be a father for a *kairos* amount of time. When that opportunity is gone, it will never come again.

The lessons my boys need to hear this spring can't be taught next year when I'm not so busy. Their teachable time—their *kairos*—will be gone. I need to be obedient today.

Number Our Days

What is the most important thing in your life? When you come to the end of your three score and 10, what do you think will be on your mind?

Numerous studies have found that the most important issue to persons facing death is their relationships with those they love. Rarely do the dying express regret over money, business opportunities, personal appearance or public achievements. Again and again the dying person is desperately concerned with his/her relationships: Have I said what needed to be said? Does she know I love her? Is he still angry with me?

There is a television commercial showing interviews of different people who were asked how they would like to be remembered. A retired football player answered this way: "I want to be remembered as a good father and a good family man." That really gripped me because that is the way I want to be remembered.

I know that I could be called by the Lord to be with Him at any moment. Now is the time to build the relationships that will be strong and secure when death eventually comes, as it must, to each of us. Now is the time to build memories, to develop communication, to experience life together. Now is the time to open ourselves and our families to the treasures that the Holy Spirit has to give us.

After concentrating on my role as a father through these past years, I know that my children will have many vivid memories of times I have spent with them. There have been times of troubles, times of fun, time during trips, ordinary times and special times. If I died this day, I have the certainty that they have abundant knowledge of their loving earthly father from which to draw an understanding of their loving heavenly Father.

A Vision and a Plan

So what changed me? God convinced me that good teaching, good principles and good intentions just weren't enough. If we were going to make specific, concrete changes in our behavior, we needed a specific, concrete *plan* to put the teachings into action.

Proverbs 29:18 *(KJV)* says, "Where there is no vision, the people perish." But I've added to that verse in the Rand Revised Version: "Without a vision the people perish, and without a plan, the vision perishes." We had a vision of what we ought to do, but we needed a plan to put the vision into action.

Two main ideas stood out as I put together the plan to move from inspiration to action. First, I felt the need to call other men to hold one another accountable to change our life-styles. This mean that we needed to have a high level of accountability to one another, emphasizing discipline while remembering grace.

Second, I realized that whatever group came together would need to be in this commitment long enough to change basic habit patterns. I placed an announcement in our Sunday bulletin and sent out the following letter to a select group of men in the congregation:

COLLEGE HILL PRESBYTERIAN CHURCH

Ron Rand
CO-PASTOR

5742 HAMILTON AVENUE
CINCINNATI, OHIO 45224
513-541-5676

Dear Fathers,

As indicated by the bulletin this past Sunday, and just like the ad for the Marines, I am looking for a few good men who are willing to work on becoming better

F—Fathers

A—Accountable

T—To

H—Healthy

E—Enduring

R—Relationships and

S—Spirituality

Qualifications include fathers who are 35-45 years of age, who have children between the ages of birth and 10 and who are willing to spend two years in study and practice in two areas:

1. Ephesians 5:25: "Husbands, love your wives, as Christ loved the church and gave himself up for her."
2. Ephesians 5:16: "Making the most of the time . . . [with children]."

I have talked with many fathers who attended the Dobson film series and were greatly inspired. But as yet, I have not found one who has been able *to specifically name a concrete change in his life*. The purpose of this two-year study is to change our life-styles as it relates to our wives and children. There will be a high level of accountability among the group. I am looking not for inspiration, *but for action*. I want to be a better husband and better father and want to get with other men who not only desire to do the same, but will count the cost and will pay the price of accomplishing this.

Some of my proposals at this stage are:
1. Set this FATHERS[3] Ministry as a priority for the next two years, with weekly meetings.
2. Assign specific reading assignments with accompanying worksheets that lead to precise action plans each week.
3. Develop accountability in specific areas, such as weekly scheduled times with spouses and children, and the development of detailed family sharing time, including fun and worship.
4. Set specific personal and family goals for a two-year period.
5. After the first year's study with one another, FATHERS will divide into small groups

and repeat the process with other men recruited by fathers in the original group.

I don't mean to scare you with all this, but I'm deeply concerned about the future of our families and the failure of our past to equip us to be effective husbands and fathers. Therefore, I want to "put my money where my mouth is" and covenant with those of like mind.

If you desire to be a part of this action, write to me, expressing in a paragraph or two why you want to be a candidate for this adventure. I am not looking for successful people, but for men who are willing to learn *to lay down their lives* for their wives and their children.

Please pray with me as to the Lord's leading in this ministry.

Sincerely in Christ,

Ron

Ron Rand, D. Min.

The members of College Hill Presbyterian Church are a curious bunch of people. The tougher the requirements are for any ministry, the larger and more determined the response. Twenty-seven men responded to this appeal! I was overwhelmed by the statements in their letters as well as by their apparent willingness to make the family their first priority. The following are some quotes from those applications:

> "I am convinced that the role of a father is the most crucial factor in determining the measure by which God's master plan for the family will be fulfilled."

> "I believe that I have the courage to confront what the world tells me I ought to be."

> "I admit that I have my life polluted with a variety of worldly responsibilities. I am questioning what the real priorities should be."

> "The word, 'disciple,' stands out and I realize what a mediocre example I am for my daughter in this area."

> "I am both excited and relieved to write this letter. I am excited because I believe the Lord wants me to get my act together. I am relieved because I can see some real direction available in doing so."

On August 5, 1981, 28 men, including myself, met and prayed together for the Lord's direction. I've never seen a group of men who were more determined to accomplish what they set out to do! They decided that we would meet at 6:03 *every* Monday morning. (Boy, were they determined!) This book will present some of the many lessons we have learned together through these years.

> Not that I have already obtained this or am already perfect; but I press on to make it my own, because Christ Jesus has made me his

own. Brethren, I do not consider that I have made it my own; but one thing I do, forgetting what lies behind and straining forward to what lies ahead, I press on toward the goal for the prize of the upward call of God in Christ Jesus. Let those of us who are mature be thus minded; and if in anything you are otherwise minded, God will reveal that also to you. Only let us hold true to what we have attained (Phil. 3:12-16).

Chapter 2

Getting to Know the Lord, Others and You!

You shall love the Lord your God with all your heart, and with all your soul, and with all your mind. This is the great and first commandment. And a second is like it, You shall love your neighbor as yourself. On these two commandments depend all the law and the prophets (Matt. 22:37-40).

In order to love the Lord, we must spend time with the Lord. This is our first priority, because there is no other way that we can become His disciples. The second priority is to love others, and in the FATHERS Ministry, this means our wives and children. There can be no "others" in our lives that need our love nearly so much. These two priorities are stated clearly in Matthew 22:37-40, but there is a third that is often overlooked: and that is to love ourselves. If we are to love others as we love ourselves, we had best know ourselves. To forgive and accept ourselves as Christ forgives and accepts us—this is the third priority.

Daily Time with the Lord

Daily time with the Lord is our first priority, so we *must* plan ahead to be sure that it happens. We think, "I'll spend an hour in prayer each day this week," but what happens? We wake up late, gulp down breakfast and rush out to work. Who has time for prayer? All day long we push and hustle to get things done on time, to punch the clock, to make the next appointment. Then we hurry home through rush-hour traffic and barely have time to read the paper before supper and the six o'clock news. Maybe we have to rush out again to the evening meeting at church, and on and on. Time for prayer? Sunday morning—maybe—if we're not too exhausted to make it to church!

We have so many things to do that the most important thing is crowded out. And it's not that we fill our time with worthless or trivial things, although that may be part of the problem. Most often the question is whether to schedule good things—or the best thing.

I remember well my first years in the ministry in a little town up in Minnesota. I was fresh out of seminary and on fire for God. I started neighborhood evangelism and youth work and everything you can imagine. And the Lord was good. He gave us fruit and that church started to grow. In 1968 the membership doubled, and in 1969 we built a new church!

Then there were more people in the little flock and they were all babes in Christ who needed to be taught and fed from the Word. So I began an Adult Sunday School program, weeknight classes and counseling sessions and I was the busiest young minister you ever saw! I was so busy doing things *for* the Lord's people that I was having less and less time *with* the Lord. Doing all the good things, I neglected the best thing: time spent with the Lord.

Recently, I was in a restaurant talking with a friend about the FATHERS Ministry. "It's easy to become a father," he said, "biologically speaking. You go through the physical actions and it just happens. But you only become a parent by being a parent. If anyone is successful at all as a parent, the key must be spending time with the Lord."

There is a vast difference between fathering a child and being a father through all the growing years. Psychologists tell us that young children form their concepts of God by what they see in their earthly fathers during the first years of life. What a responsibility! How can we meet such expectations? The only way to learn to be a father is to draw continually closer to the Father of fathers and learn to be like Him.

Four Key Points

In progressing from good intentions to changed behavior, FATHERS found that there are four key points to keep us moving toward success:

Set a Time

Face it. If you don't set a definite time for prayer, just like a definite time to go to work, watch a ball game or meet an appointment at the dentist, you just won't pray.

Someone is sure to say, "I don't like to be legalistic about these things. I don't want to be too rigid. I want to be free to pray when the Spirit moves me." I can appreciate that point of view. Yet in my own life and in the lives of other FATHERS members, things just don't happen unless they are planned.

For example, if I am going overseas I could pack a bag, buy my ticket and hop on the plane, but I wouldn't get very far. To travel outside the United States I must also go to the post office, apply for a passport, apply for a visa, get certain shots and all those things. I can't "just go with the flow." There are certain things in life that you have to plan for or they just don't happen.

Some people resist sitting down with a Bible to pray because of the term "quiet time." They think they have to sit and be bored for 20 minutes in order to be "spiritual." That's a major misunderstanding! Let's get rid of the term quiet time. The time I spend each morning is anything but quiet because the Holy Spirit is so active. Much time is spent listening as the Spirit gives a new perspective on the day ahead, directions for my work in the office and insights about my time with Jennifer and the children. When I'm not listening to His voice, I'm actively reading and writing or singing and praying.

One image given in the Scriptures of our relationship with God is that of husband and wife. If I get up and don't talk with Jennifer in the morning, our relationship is strained by evening. It's the same with our relationship with the Lord. We need to have opportunities to talk with one another.

Or we could use the image of a baseball player who has been injured and sits on the bench for six weeks because he has lost his "eye" for the ball. An athlete needs to be in constant training to keep sharp. Time with the Lord is also a discipline and we need constant practice to keep in shape.

When a day goes by without prayer, as will happen

because we aren't perfect, we confess it as sin, accept forgiveness and go on. Don't let the feeling of stale guilt spoil the fresh bread of the Word when you again have time with the Lord. As the Shorter Catechism says, "The chief end of man is to glorify God and enjoy Him forever." Enjoy Him!

Involve Accountability

Each member of FATHERS is accountable to report to his buddy (prayer partner) every week and days when prayer time is skipped *must* be accounted for. If I know I will have to explain to my buddy why I decided to sleep another 15 minutes instead of getting up to pray, it might just move me out of bed!

Buddies also report on meaningful aspects of our prayers. (We soon realized that it isn't much good to stumble out of bed at 5:30 A.M., only to stare bleary-eyed at a blank notebook.) The idea is to hold each other accountable in the consistency of prayer and also in the content and quality of prayer.

There are various support groups like Weight Watchers and Alcoholics Anonymous that are built on the concept of mutual accountability. These groups all recognize that it's hard to change behavior alone. For alcoholics and those involved in other forms of chemical abuse, it's virtually impossible. But in a group where every member understands and shares the same difficulty, suddenly it becomes possible to believe that behavior can change. When there is a buddy depending on you for support and who is supporting you, there can be a concrete change.

Expect Interruptions

Even though occasional interruptions must be

expected, hold the time sacred. One good reason for praying early in the morning is that the phone isn't likely to ring. There's not much on television and the wife and kids are still asleep. (If there's an infant in your house you could be walking the baby and giving Mommy some rest while meditating on how patient the heavenly Father is with you.)

Going back to Moses, we see that he was interrupted in his time with God up on Mount Sinai. There he was, in the greatest "mountaintop experience" of his life and he was interrupted. "Go, get down! For your people whom you brought out of the land of Egypt have corrupted themselves" (Exod. 32:7, *NKJV*). We should learn from Moses' way of handling his interruptions—he prayed for the people who interrupted him! (See Exod. 32:11-14.)

Have a Daily Devotional Plan

Use some meaningful, challenging material for your prayer time. Some folks get along fine with just their Bible and a notebook, but most of us need some additional help in gathering insights through a study guide or a devotional of some sort.

A specific formula for establishing prayer and study habits can often be helpful. David Lowry, a leader in our presbytery, uses this plan: one hour each day, one day each month and one week each year. On the monthly "prayer day" and during his yearly "prayer week," David spends time in fasting, study and deeper contemplative prayer. Another formula is to pray one minute a day for each year of your age. If I am 43 years old, I will spend 43 minutes in prayer each day.

Another good suggestion is to take time to write down each prayer request. An inexpensive spiral-bound notebook works just fine. Write down the date and the request and keep praying for that item, thanking God that He is in the process of answering until the answer comes. Then record the answer and the date. This is the best way I know of teaching theology to yourself and to your children. You are teaching the reality of God's presence and concern for our needs as you see the clear results of your prayers.

I hope you are catching the idea that time with the Lord is more than a daily ritual. It is more than a set of "do's and don'ts," more than one hour set aside to "be spiritual." It is a personal relationship. One day it might mean spending an hour in prayer or it may be five minutes—just long enough to get a "hug" from the Lord and an uplift by the Spirit. The length of time and the method used is only important insofar as to discipline ourselves.

Getting to Know Ourselves

Our first FATHERS group first used the devotional *This Morning with God.*[1] Most of us thrived on that format, but two or three fathers preferred something more flexible. They were ready to try something different right away and for a while we figured that these guys were real tough cases in the discipline department. Then our pastor of counseling suggested that we might each benefit by taking a "personal preference" test. We agreed and were amazed at the insights we gained and applied directly to our devotional lives, our marriage relationships, and our families. This understanding has become such a valuable aspect of FATHERS that it needs to be discussed in some detail here.

The Myers-Briggs Personality Preference Indicator is a series of questions that discerns specific preferences indicating various types of personalities. There are four areas of preferences:

Extrovert (E)	or	**Introvert (I)**
Outgoing: People-person		Inward: Private-person
Sensing (S)	or	**Intuitive (N)**
Practical: "This is the way it is."		Probable: "This is the way it could be."
Thinking (T)	or	**Feeling (F)**
Factualize: "Just the facts please, mam."		Personalize: "It just moved me so deeply!"
Judging (J)	or	**Perceptive (P)**
Closer: "Let's close the deal."		Opener: "Let's keep looking."

The preferences indicate a person's profile or "type," designated by the initials of the four areas. (For example, three different individuals' types might be *ESTJ, ISFJ* or *ISTJ*.) There is *no* right or wrong type—only individual differences. One person with an introvert preference may prefer to relax by working alone in the workshop, while another with an extrovert preference may relax by joining others for a game of softball. A *J* feels comfortable with carefully scheduled and predictable events, while a *P* would rather be spontaneous and do something when "in the mood." Let's look at two apostles with opposite personality types.

Apostolic Types

James was concerned with works or behavior (see Jas. 2:14), with judging (see 3:1) and with being steadfast (see 5:9-11). Without jumping to conclusions, it seems likely that Saint James was a Sensory Judger. We could use the words "Steadfast Justice" to characterize Saint James, the "SJ."

Now let's look at Paul. In Romans 5:1, he emphasizes the fact that we are justified by faith and in Philippians 4:11-12, Paul witnesses that he can be content "in whatever state I am"—he can "go with the flow." So we might use the words, "Faith and Peace" to characterize Father Paul, the Feeling Perceiver or "FP."

On November sixteenth, we distributed the Myers-Briggs Personality Preference Indicator to each FATHERS member with an extra copy for each spouse. The forms were analyzed and returned two weeks later and we began to learn a lot about ourselves, how we relate to one another, and how we relate to different forms of study and prayer.

It turned out that almost all of the men in the group were *SJ*s: 24 out of 27! We are the sensory judgers, Steadfast Judgment people, like Saint James. We prefer schedules and plans and are more comfortable with facts and figures than with feelings and fantasy. But two or three men had profiles indicating a preference for spontaneity and less structure. They are Faith and Peace people, like Father Paul. Guess which types had difficulty with *This Morning with God*? Exactly—the *FP*s.

Different personality types respond to different stimuli. *SJ*s like prescribed study. *NP*s are more inclined to be spontaneous and unscheduled, able to go with the flow of their own thoughts as they read or pray. Although most studies (in fact, most of our American educational systems) are geared for the *SJ* personality, neither type is right or wrong. Both types can benefit from the other in working toward a balance: *SJ*s can become more flexible, *NP*s more systematized.

31

Applying Knowledge to Prayer

There are different forms of prayer that can give freedom to differing personality types. Imaging is a style or form of prayer that can be meaningful to persons who struggle with structured study guides. Read the story of the disciples in the storm from Mark 4. Imagine yourself in the boat. How do you feel while Jesus is sleeping? What do you think when He stills the storm? Record your thoughts and feelings.

Another style of prayer might be to take a verse like John 3:16 or 1 John 1:9 and replace the impersonal pronouns with your own name. How does the new reading change the meaning of the verse for you?

Experiment with various forms of prayer, both to find what is most meaningful to you and to grow in understanding ways that seemed uncomfortable to you before. The book *Please Understand Me: Character and Temperament Types*[2] was made available to all fathers who wished to do further study in learning about different personality types.

Getting to Know Others: Our Wives

When the FATHERS members took the Myers-Briggs Personality Preference Indicator, we also asked our wives to participate. We discovered things about our spouses that we had ignored or taken for granted for years. Differences that had been sources of friction and arguments took on a new light. Mysteries—"Why do you always do such-and-such when I want to do so-and-so?"—became less irritating and more acceptable. Suddenly many of the quirks that had come up in our relationships over the years had rational explanations.

For example, one wife said that for many years she

had dreaded the "fellowship hour" after church each Sunday morning. Her husband would spend 15 or 20 minutes cruising the foyer and fellowship hall, chatting and visiting and looking up friends, while she felt lost in a swirling ocean of strangers. (Our congregation is very large. In fact, hundreds of individuals mingle between services.) She thought that she must be imagining it all and that she should stop feeling so "silly."

After taking the Myers-Briggs, this woman realized what was happening: she is an intuitive introvert—an *INFP*—so it was no wonder that she had difficulty functioning in a crowd. Her husband, on the other hand, is an extrovert and is in his element when in a crowd. This couple agreed that he could have his time of fellowshipping while she waited with one or two friends in the church library.

Another common discovery concerned the decision-making process. One spouse would look at the facts (sensory/thinker) while the other was feeling out the situation (intuitive/feeler). Conversations such as, "I've explained all the facts. Why can't you make up your mind?" or "I don't know, Honey, but it just doesn't feel right!" began to make more sense. Issues that used to lead to arguments and conflict could now be handled with consideration: "She needs to gather more information" or "He doesn't feel comfortable yet, so we'll consider some other options."

Do you really know your wife? Do you understand how her mind works, why she feels one way at one time but not at another? Would you like to know her better? Would you like to be able to understand the way she thinks and what makes her unique? She really is a special person, a one-of-a-kind creation of the Master Artist. A personal preference indicator such as the Myers-Briggs can be a wonderful tool in growing closer together and deeper in love.

Or, as FATHERS member Roger says, "Praise the Lord for your wife, just the way she isn't!"

There are two points to remember about personality preferences:

1. There is a difference between personality and type. You may have the same *type* of preference as another person, but an entirely different personality. Each individual is special and unique and the Myers-Briggs Indicator is only one tool for understanding one another.

2. Types may change over a period of time. It's helpful to repeat the test periodically, hoping to see growth in weaker areas. For example, if someone now scores 22 in "thinking" and 2 in "feeling," that person could strive to grow in the "feeling" area.

But I offer a caution: Once you have discovered your mate's type, don't put her (or anyone else) in a box, saying, "Well, she's an *ISFP*, so that's why she acts that way." In the same sense, because you are a particular type does not allow you to think that's the way you're destined to be: "Well, you know, I'm not a feeler, so therefore I can't be expected to express my feelings." Nonsense!

One FATHERS member testified that both his own and his wife's types changed dramatically in about a year. He had learned to take the lead in decision-making and planning for the family—a role his wife had previously been forced to play. Now both feel that they are understood and have greater freedom to respond according to preference instead of acting out "what we're supposed to do." Praise the Lord!

Getting to Know Others: Our Kids

The Myers-Briggs Indicator can be a great help in understanding our kids. Studies indicate that most individuals tend to be extroverted, so we think of that preference as normal. Understanding various personality preference possibilities helps relieve many parental puzzlements.

Joshua, our eldest, is very creative. He processes things internally before he responds, while the younger boys process while they are speaking. Josh is very competitive, playing to win. Nathan is less competitive, playing games mainly for the pleasure of being with friends. Christopher, the youngest, is a natural entertainer; he loves to show off in front of others. Maybe he'll grow up to be a preacher like his dad.

Jennifer and I are both extroverted. We want to grab the kids right off the school bus and talk about their day. That's fine with Nathan, who is bursting to share all his experiences and problems, but not Josh. He wants to come home and be alone in his room for a while, to look at his papers and just unwind. After a little while he'll come downstairs, make himself a snack and then he's ready to talk.

It would be so easy for us to frustrate Josh by interpreting his behavior as hostility and expecting him to be extroverted like ourselves and his brothers. Understanding that there can be different preferences because of different personality types allows us to appreciate Joshua as an individual.

Other preferences, including sensory/intuitive, thinking/feeling and judging/perceiving, are not usually pronounced until children reach their high school years. But in some children there are definite preferences right away. You may have a child who is always asking, "What are we doing this afternoon? And then what are we doing tonight? And what are we doing next Tuesday?" This is the little *SJ* speaking, looking for that agenda, the scheduled events. She may become angry when plans are changed without warning. Or perhaps she just can't tolerate surprises.

Another child may not like scheduled events to interrupt free time—even when those events occur every week, on the same day, at the same time. It seems strange that the child would not expect and accept a regular schedule. Yet every week it comes as an interference: "But I don't want to go to choir, now, I'm still playing with my racetrack!" This is probably the same child who can "go with the flow" and who enjoys surprises. He is probably an *FP*, moving by moods and feelings.

Even without using a formal analysis like the Myers-Briggs Indicator, it is immeasurably helpful to recognize that there are multiple differences among individuals that have nothing to do with right and wrong or good or bad— they are simply differences.

I like to rub Josh's back at bedtime and I often use this quiet moment together to ask what was the best thing that happened to him that day. It seems like two hours before he answers. In reality it is probably about 45 seconds, but I'll get impatient and repeat, "Josh, *tell* me about your day!"

My mind works in such a way that *I* usually answer questions with a quick response, saying the first thing that comes to mind. But Josh is different. He needs time for his mental computer to access the files, calculate and produce output: "Let's see, strawberries for breakfast (mental disk drives are turning) . . . friends on the ball field (buzz, whir, access new file) . . . softball practice . . . ah, yes, the best thing happened at lunch . . . . " He took my question seriously and needed a moment to answer me truthfully.

Learning that it is possible for my son's thought processes to respond differently than my own helps me to modify my expectations and to be patient.[3]

The FATHERS Oath

From these basic principles of knowing and loving the Lord, ourselves and our families, the following oath was formed, memorized and repeated at the beginning of each meeting. Again and again, individual fathers testify that repeating the oath together has been a deeply meaningful experience—especially occasions when we stand in a circle, raise our Bibles and make this pledge in the presence of our families:

On my honor, I will do my best to present myself to God as one approved, a workman who has no need to be ashamed, rightly handling the Word of Truth.[4]

I will love my wife as Christ loved the church and gave Himself up for her.[5]

I will not provoke my children to anger but will bring them up in the discipline and discipleship of the Lord Jesus Christ.[6]

I will receive the Word of God in my heart daily and will teach it diligently to my children and shall talk of it when I sit in my house and when I walk by the way, and when I lie down, and when I rise.[7]

As for me and my house, we will serve the Lord.[8]

For I can do all these things through Christ who strengthens me.[9]

Tips

Family Response Verses may be used in greeting one another, when leaving for school or work, at bedtime or mealtime, etc.

Each family member memorizes the verses.
Each family practices on a daily basis.
Each family may reverse the responses.
Responses may be used in squad meetings[10] as well as in families.

Psalm 118:24

Parents: This is the day which the LORD has made;
Children: Let us rejoice and be glad in it.

Genesis 31:44,49

Parents: Come now, let us make a covenant, you and I; and let it be a witness between you and me.
Children: The Lord watch between you and me when we are absent one from the other.

2 Corinthians 13:14

Father: The grace of the Lord Jesus Christ
Mother: and the love of God the Father
Children: and the fellowship of the Holy Spirit be with [us] all.

Philippians 4:13

Parents: I can do all things
Children: in [Christ] who strengthens me.

Psalm 67:1

 Parents: May God be gracious to us and
   bless us
 Children: and make his face to shine upon us.

Numbers 6:24-26

 Father: The LORD bless you and keep you:
 Mother: The LORD make his face to shine upon
   you, and be gracious to you:
 Children: The LORD lift up his countenance
   upon you, and give you peace.

Children should be encouraged to pray at meals and use as the basis of their prayers favorite Bible passages or other memorized passages. This causes variety in the mealtime thanksgiving prayers and promotes incorporation of these verses in everyday life.

Chapter 3

How to Share Your Schedules

*For everything there is a season, and
a time for every matter under heaven:
a time to be born, and a time to die;
a time to plant, and a time to pluck up
what is planted;
a time to kill, and a time to heal;
a time to break down, and a time to
build up;
a time to weep, and a time to laugh;
a time to mourn, and a time to dance;
a time to cast away stones, and a time
to gather stones together;
a time to embrace, and a time to
refrain from embracing;
a time to seek, and a time to lose;
a time to keep, and a time to cast
away;
a time to rend, and a time to sew;*

a time to keep silence, and a time to speak;
a time to love, and a time to hate;
a time for war, and a time for peace.
What gain has the worker from his toil? (Eccles. 3:1-9).

If there is one key to the success of the FATHERS Ministry, it is learning to manage time by sharing schedules with our wives. The concept is simple. On Sunday afternoon or evening, each FATHERS member and his wife sit down with a calendar and share every activity each of them have for every day of the week. Everything is listed: job schedules, church activities, social functions, the children's school activities—everything. Shopping trips, visits from friends and relatives and appointments at the doctor or dentist all go onto one family calendar.

Scheduling, the key to success? Aw, c'mon, now, preacher! No! I'm serious, because we've seen over and over again how important sharing our schedules with our families really is.

Time

Our ways are many and we are involved in so many kinds of things. And our ways are different: each child is different, each person is different, each mate is different. To have time with each family member, to build relationships and to have control over time instead of being controlled by time—this is the secret of scheduling. Urgent events will always come up, but we have learned *how* to maintain control, and therefore, maintain peace. Sharing

42

your schedules can be God's way of giving you peace at all times.

On the other hand, nothing gets me into more trouble than failing to share my schedule with my family. In fact, probably the worst thing I ever did to Jennifer happened because I tried to accomplish too many things in too little time. I became wrapped up in my own plans and neglected to give Jennifer the information she needed—creating a terrible mess.

In the summer of 1985 I was preparing to leave for South Africa. My flight left on Saturday morning and it had been one of those hectic weeks. On Friday I noticed that the tree cutters were doing some work for my neighbor, so I went over and asked if they could be back in this neighborhood soon to cut my trees. They said that we were on the schedule and perhaps they could even cut our trees the next day (which was the day I was to leave for South Africa). I said that would be wonderful and I would mark the trees with yellow paint: *T* for trim and *C* for cut.

Bright and early Saturday morning we were wakened by the sound of buzz saws and trees crashing. Before I knew it, Jennifer came running in crying, "You've cut down my favorite tree!"

I snapped awake. "What do you mean?"

She said, "You had those men cut down my favorite tree, my most beautiful tree! Why did you have them cut it down?"

As I pulled on some clothes, I said, "They must have read my marks wrong! I marked that tree to be trimmed." But when we went outside and stared at the pile of firewood that used to be Jennifer's beautiful tree, one of the pieces was clearly marked with a yellow *C*.

Jennifer was crushed. "Why didn't you tell me the men were coming to cut down the trees? Why didn't you ask

43

me to make sure which were to be cut and which were to be trimmed?"

I knew then how George Washington must have felt! *I could not tell a lie*, either. Number one, I failed to tell Jennifer I had talked to the men on Friday. Number two, I failed to consult her about the trees to be cut. Combining the sound of the buzz saws and the shock of finding her favorite tree cut with the normal tension in our home (because of my need to pack and get to the airport) produced the same result: we both felt terrible. It wasn't a nice send-off for my trip to South Africa and I had to do some quick asking for forgiveness before I could go in peace. I was wise enough, also, to call from the airport to make sure that everything was still in order.

Jennifer and other wives have voiced unanimous agreement that communicating weekly schedules is vital. FATHERS' emphasis on disciplining ourselves to really communicate in our scheduling has worked toward the goal of making important decisions together. Any number of FATHERS members and their wives can testify how essential it is to share schedules and how disastrous it is when we fail!

The Three *D*s: Three Aspects of Weekly Scheduling

Let's look into three aspects of our scheduling—the three *D*s—so that it is clear why this principle has made such a difference in our lives. These three *D*s must be included in any scheduling time.

The First *D*: Discussion
Discussion is simply giving one another the facts about what is planned. This step may seem too obvious to for-

get, yet it happens all too frequently. And failure to discuss is a real pitfall for all concerned. Spouses need all the facts—and any revisions that occur as soon as they occur.

I had made arrangements for Jennifer and me to speak on marital intimacy at a meeting of young married couples. I came home after church one Sunday, about six weeks later, and there was Jennifer holding the church bulletin. She smiled sweetly at me. "Oh, Ron, it's so nice to read in the bulletin that Rev. Rand and Jennifer are speaking next week at the Young Marrieds' meeting. Are you going to do this alone or did you have some other Jennifer in mind?" I had failed to share the calendar and she was expressing her opinions with self-control and creativity.

The Second *D*: Dialoguing

Dialoguing simply means responding with opinions and feelings related to the facts. It is sharing on a personal level rather than on a factual level.

We often have various ministry meetings in our home. It seems to help relationships to invite lay persons to the pastor's home to get to know one another as people and find out that the preacher's kids are down to earth and real as they run through the living room fussing at one another and fighting—it's very eye-opening. On one occasion when I wanted to schedule a group in our home, Jennifer and I sat down to discuss and to dialogue when the meeting should be. In discussing the facts, it seemed right to arrange the meeting on a certain evening. But as we dialogued, we remembered how other evening meetings had been interrupted when our boys went to bed. Our living room is right next to their bedrooms and the boys shared how they were kept awake by the conversations. Through sharing our opinions and feelings, we saw that evening group meetings were not the best for our family. So now we try to invite people on Sunday afternoons when all of our schedules are more free.

As we were working on this chapter together, Jennifer pointed out that she and I used to have much more dialogue before we had children because there was just the two of us. With each new child, we found it was more difficult to share feelings because the variables were multiplied and the arrangements were more complicated.

Then as the children grew older, we saw the absolute necessity of sitting down and sharing our schedules *with* them. It often becomes a problem of juggling a schedule of several different choirs, scout meetings, basketball, youth groups, deacons meetings, dental appointments, etc. It is all too easy to slip into allowing separate decisions to be made by the wife or husband without the other's input. Or perhaps we share information without checking out one another's feelings. Then we find ourselves announcing what will happen rather than dialoguing. We often miscommunicate because we fail to check feelings as well as facts.

The Third *D*: Decisions

Discussion gives the facts, leading to dialogue, giving feelings and opinions. Then the way is clear for the third *D*: appropriate *decisions*.

Sooner or later it becomes apparent that the choices we have to make are not really between good and bad or good and better, but between better and best—especially if you have different kids with different interests. One child might be interested in soccer, another in baseball, another in music. As our kids enter the teenage years we realize that they want to have impromptu parties and are always in the process of choosing.

Because Jennifer and I are able to use this process of discussion, dialogue and decision, we are able to maintain reasonable limitations on the boys' activities, time spent with friends and our family times.

Our entire family is involved in baseball. Some of the games are played at the same sports complex where there are four different fields, but occasionally a game is scheduled on the same morning in another part of town. If this occurs I am often tied down as a manager at one game area with one child and Jennifer is at another area with child number two. This means that number three child's game is elsewhere and he does not have his parents watching him play that day. Yet he can accept this without feeling neglected because he knows that his turn will come the next week. Scheduling can help do that.

Extra Help

Take advantage of the various tools available commercially for planning and scheduling efficiently. Most FATHERS members carry a pocket appointment calendar with them and keep a family calendar at home on the refrigerator or beside the telephone. The trick is matching both calendars daily. One father says that he programs his schedule on his home computer. His kids enjoy working with the computer, so they take advantage of every opportunity to update the calendar and keep the family schedule straight.

This past Christmas I purchased a "Cincinnati" calendar, listing the major cultural, regional and sports events happening in Cincinnati. Because of our lack in planning, we used to miss most of the special events at the stadium or the Cincinnati Gardens, the circuses or the various festivals held in town. Now this calendar alerts us to the activities that are coming up and we can plan ahead.

Our boys always wanted to go to the mud racing at the Colosseum. The center of the Colosseum is made into a sea of mud and these big cars, heavy trucks and motorcycles have to go through the mud. Boy, oh, boy, the kids wanted to see that! Mud racing isn't high on Jennifer's list of spectator sports so it didn't get top priority in our planning. This year, with the Cincinnati calendar, the boys made certain that mud racing was written in as a family event—nothing was to be scheduled on that night. But on the night of the races a last-minute conflict came up in my schedule, as happens so often to a pastor. I thought to ask a young man who had been a counselor at the boys' summer camp to take them to the races and that pleased the boys enormously. So Jennifer and I enjoyed the serendipity of going out alone that night after my evening appointment, while the boys went to mud racing with their special friend from camp.

The Four Good Fruits

What are the fruits of discussing your schedules together? I suggest four.

The Best Choices

First of all, it allows us to make the best possible *choices*. We are able to look at and discuss all the facts from each point of view. Then we can dialogue our own feelings and find out how important these things really are.

This has become more important since Joshua has become a teenager. It allows him to really share his own feelings and to make his own choices. Recently there was a Young Life all-night bowling party. Originally, he planned to go to a friend's home that afternoon, bowl all night, return to his friend's home and sleep Saturday morning, then go together to another friend's birthday party that was going to be celebrated on Saturday evening. Because each of these parties was located in the part of town where the boys attend school, Joshua's plan was actually very considerate of his parents, saving several hours of driving time.

But past experience has shown that a lack of sleep really wears on Joshua, making him queasy as well as generally grumpy and run-down. As we sat together and looked at all the facts, we shared in dialogue our appreciation for his plan—which eliminated our need to drive back and forth. We also discussed whether or not he could rest at this friend's home. I said that I would be glad to do the extra driving if he chose to come home to rest.

Joshua was able to come to his own decision that he would come on home after school to eat and get a few hours sleep. Later I drove him to the bowling party, then picked him up again at six A.M. He slept until noon on Saturday and realized that going to another party that evening would not be a good thing. His friend, on the other hand, did not rest, went to both parties and felt terrible at school the next week. Josh felt good and we felt good, proud of our son's ability to make sound decisions.

Eliminates Conflict

So the first fruit of scheduling is the ability to make the best choices. Secondly, I think it eliminates *conflict* by preventing unpleasant surprises.

In a recent book entitled *Parent Burnout,* author and professor Joseph Procaccini of Loyola University calls mothering "the quintessential stressful role because the essence of stress is change."[1] He makes a comparison between mothers and another high-stress profession: air-traffic controllers. Most people assume that air-traffic controllers experience stress on account of the awesome responsibility of guiding airliners through congested traffic patterns over urban airports. But the professor says that the primary source of their stress is the constantly changing conditions the controllers must manage.

"Air-traffic controllers constantly need to adjust to new realities," Dr. Procaccini writes. "They must stay intensely connected to those realities because the stakes are so high."[2] For instance, at 7:00 A.M. there may be three private planes approaching and two 747s on the runway waiting to go out. The winds are variable, visibility is good. But two minutes later, at 7:02, the wind may be calm and visibility is limited. This presents a totally new configuration of aircraft on the ground and in the air.

A mother's situation is likewise one of constant change: first the children are in the backyard for five minutes, then they are running through the house. Next the phone rings, the baby wails and the dog throws up on the carpet. The emotional climate in a household can range from joyful to tragic from one minute to the next. While scheduling cannot eliminate all of this confusion, it can control many other major stress factors.

Traditionally, we invite the laypeople who share the evangelism ministry with me to our home for a holiday celebration. I had scheduled a time for that on my calendar, but neglected to copy that event onto our home calendar. It turned out that on the scheduled date Jennifer was to be in Minnesota with her dad. So when we sat down to share, I opened with my usual introductory remark: "Oh, by the way . . . . " When Jennifer hears, "Oh, by the way," she knows there is trouble ahead.

When I confessed the problem, I was very efficient in discussing the facts. Jennifer was ready to go into the dialogue phase by sharing her feelings: "Okay, Mr. Organizer, how are we going to do this?"

Of course, Jennifer normally takes care of all the

decoration—the little treats and goodies and so forth that make hospitality so much fun. She also knew that after several days without her attention, the house would be in no condition for entertaining guests. We worked through the dialogue and agreed that the people from the evangelism ministry would be contacted and we would explain the situation. Instead of canceling the get-together, some members would come early to help prepare and decorate the house, other people would bring various goodies and some would stay late to clean up. So that's the way it was. Jennifer went to Minnesota and the evangelism people took responsibility for their party. We all had a good time with minimal stress.

Encourages Accountability

Third, making schedules together encourages *accountability* in each family member. This is so important, especially when you have three kids tugging at your legs saying, "Dad, can I do this, can I do that?" When we sit down to make our schedules, Jennifer and I first share with each other. Then we bring the boys in to discuss and dialogue so they can discover times when we can do things with them. We write their times down on the calendar itself and it enables them to make choices.

Suppose that Christopher and I have planned to go to the comic shop after school. He comes home that particular day, saying that he and his friend want to play baseball. I can remind him, "Chris, this is the time we set aside to visit the comic shop. Do you want to change this?"

He might say, "Dad, I really want to play ball. Can we go some other time?"

I will say, "Yes, but it might be another week before we can have that time." So then the next day, if Christopher begins to complain that we've not had time together, I can remind him that we renegotiated. Then he learns the importance of our having that time and the importance of his own decision to change that time.

A Foundation for Communication

A fourth fruit of scheduling is that it lays a basis for *communication* to really share one's feelings.

As the baseball season was coming on, Joshua and I planned to go to the Batting Cage. This is a commercial sports area where they provide a pitching machine that will pitch 30 balls at different speeds. For a certain number of tokens you can practice your batting. It really looked good for us to do that. I'd heard that this is where Pete Rose goes to practice in the off seasons and that we might see a lot of the professional players there. As we got into the car to go, there was a resistance on Josh's part. When I encouraged him to talk he asked about the cage and whether other people would be watching. What if he swung and missed? Would people laugh?

I said, "Thanks for sharing your feelings. I didn't think about that possibility. How would you feel if we just checked it out? We don't have to bat at all if we don't want to."

Joshua was open to that and that's what we did. Two weeks later he said, "Let's look at the calendar and see when we can go and bat." So it was very important for him to be able to share his feelings and to know that he had the privilege of making his own decision in a new situation.

Tips

Purchase Pocket Calendars and a Bulletin Board-type Calendar. Set a weekly time to review personal and family calendars for the upcoming week or two. Mark the dates of individual and family involvements on each. You may wish to color code these calendars according to each individual. Place the bulletin board calendar in a place near a family phone or family gathering place so it can be easily referred to when needed. The pocket calendars are to be carried by both spouses when they are away from home.

Put Weekly Times with Each Family Member on the Calendars. It is helpful for each child to know his/her planned time with each parent. This will help build important memories for each child and help the parents to say no to spontaneous requests from others outside the home.

Do Some Long-Range Planning for Special Events. Select future vacation dates and circle them in green to symbolize a "growing " time together or the "go" away time. Select future overnight or weekend mini-honeymoons. The principle: Behind every successful future date is successful present planning.

Teach and Practice the Principle of "Look Before You Leap." Teach your children to respond to phone calls or requests from friends by looking at the calendar first before responding affirmatively or negatively to sudden requests. This will help prevent future conflicts.

TAKING INVENTORY

1. How well do you know your family's schedule? Try to summarize their weekly schedule, day by day. Are there regular dental or medical check-up times?

2. In what weekly family situations or events are you functioning as (a) an active participant, and (b) a pas-

sive spectator? Is there a desire to reshuffle or change some things?

3. Think about the goals you would like to accomplish for yourself and your family within the next five years. Jot down some action steps to fulfillment of each. Share them with your family and put them on your calendar.

4. Analyze your weekly and monthly schedules. How much time are you devoting in each of the following areas: time with the Lord, time with each family member, time at work, time for yourself. Do this for four weeks in a row to discover where and how you are spending your time.

5. Is there anything specific you need to accomplish with your wife and/or children this week? Have you promised to do something with them? What past promises or expectations have yet to be fulfilled? Perhaps you can do that this week.

6. Do you ever put your plans aside to facilitate your wife's plans? In what specific ways are you concerned about her being able to meet her scheduled commitments as you are about your own?

7. Do you ever turn down adult social or recreational events to preserve family time? Are children's schedules too full?

8. Do you have a visible family calendar? How successful have you been in long-range (three-six mos.) planning for your family?

Chapter 4

What About Your Children's Mom?

Her children rise up and call her blessed;
her husband also, and he praises her
(Prov. 31:28).

We took an informal poll in our FATHERS Ministry: How many of you go jogging or play group sports? How often do you go to conventions or seminars? How often do you get to meet with partners or competitors? Most of the fathers did these things daily, weekly or at least "often." Then we asked their wives the same questions. Seldom did the women participate in jogging or group sports. Attending conventions or seminars almost never occurred. Mixing with partners or competitors (unless the wife worked outside the home) occurred maybe twice a week—at church.

In some families it is the man who receives the paycheck as a tangible reward for his labor. He may receive commendations from his superior or a promotion and a raise. But what about the woman who is a wife, mom and homemaker? There is no paycheck to acknowledge keeping the house clean, no badge saying, "Mother of the Month." Instead, *she* is the one who says, "Dad's had a rough day at the office" or "Don't bother your father"—as though we men deserve rest and quiet after a hard day's work. Shouldn't the women expect the same consideration?

How much recognition does a homemaker and mother receive? When a husband and wife are introduced to someone, the man is commonly identified by his occupation: "Hi, this is Dan Jones and he's in insurance." How often does the conversation turn to the wife with the question, "Do you work?"

Think about it. No one asks a man, "Do you work?" It is assumed he is gainfully employed or the subject is tactfully avoided. But the question is often posed to women and it implies that a homemaker does not work—at least not in the sense that the husband or career woman works. If the woman is hesitant to speak up on her behalf, her husband can deflect the blow with a strong defense: "Of course she works!" Never allow your wife to denigrate herself by murmuring, "No, I'm just a housewife." If we don't give our own wives recognition, they often won't get any.

Every homemaker needs time to get away from the house and the kids and to spend time (and a little money) on herself. Many churches have "Mother's Day Out" programs each week and most will excuse the fee for families experiencing financial stress. Two hours of peace and quiet to sit in the library, walk in the park or have a cup of coffee with a friend can make a frazzled mommie feel like a human being again. A few dollars invested in makeup or pretty lingerie could save many dollars spent at the doctor's office or on aspirins and tranquilizers! The same is true for the older moms and grandmas who don't get out of the house for fun at least once every week.

Thanks, Lord, I Needed That!

Let's go back and examine the time I began having dates (or clubtimes, as the kids say) with Jennifer. I had taken a team of laypersons to an evangelism clinic in St. Louis in October 1976, not long after Nathan's birth. While the teams went out to make calls in the community, I stayed behind with another team member, Marge Opp, to pray for the callers. The Lord began to speak to me about my marriage, instead.

"Yes, Lord," I prayed, "thank you for blessing my family. But Marge and I want to pray for the evangelism teams."

"No, Ron," said the Lord, "we need to talk about your marriage. Do you remember what day this is?"

It was October 10, Jennifer's birthday. "Well, Lord, Jennifer understands that I need to be away for this clinic. I mean, I have a very important ministry." I thought maybe God wasn't looking at the right side of this issue. "Jennifer knows that I love her."

"How does she know that?" God asked.

I thought that was a funny question. "Of course she knows I love her."

He wouldn't let me off the hook. "What does Jennifer do when it's *your* birthday, Ron?"

I thought about the celebration Jennifer arranges every year, complete with cake and cards and gifts "from the boys" which she engineers. Yes, birthdays are definitely significant to Jennifer. But I had put out no effort to make this day special for *her*. In fact, I was about as far away from her today as I could get. I tried to change the subject: "Well, she's busy now with the new baby."

"She certainly is," God agreed. "When was the last time you got her out of the house for a little fun?"

"But God," I squirmed, "you know how tight our budget is. We're tithing, you know (as if that should earn points in my favor). And we've been giving to missions as much as we possibly can. There isn't anything left for selfish luxuries."

"Selfish, Ron? Is it selfish to make your wife feel special?"

I was very uncomfortable by this time. Marge couldn't help but notice and she asked what I was thinking.

"Uh, it seems God wants to talk about my wife instead of about the evangelism teams." I shared what the Lord seemed to be saying and believe it or not, Marge agreed with God!

We talked about Jennifer, her work with the boys and about my being away from the home so often. We decided that the greatest gift I could give Jennifer was the gift of my time. I found a pen and some paper right then and wrote to her, promising that I would seek some way to give her at least one evening each week.

Marge decided to be a part of that birthday gift. She also made a gift of her time by offering to baby-sit at least one day a week so Jennifer and I could go out together. Since that day we date on a weekly basis. The responsibility is mine, not Jennifer's, to contact Marge and arrange the time. (And Marge will remind me if I fail to call her first!)

Dating Rewards

There are two principles that I have learned through this experience. First, the Lord used that special birthday, when I was away from home, to awaken my need to know and understand Jennifer. He convicted me of my insensitivity to her needs. I also realized that I must call on other FATHERS members to continue to remind me of my tendency to fall back into insensitivity. We need to hold each other accountable.

Second, the Lord provided two means to meet that need and He began with Marge Opp. Next, when Jennifer and I made the commitment to make time to be together, we soon discovered ways to enjoy our dates without breaking the budget. I also depend on other FATHERS members to help provide fresh dating ideas, the means and the motivation.

Jennifer and I discovered that we could have lunch at nice restaurants for about half the cost of an evening meal. Another father has taken advantage of "early bird specials" (dinners that are less expensive before 6:00 P.M.) offered at some dining places. One couple enjoys a breakfast together each week. We have learned that the surroundings and meal aren't nearly as important as the time to communicate and enjoy being together.

Sharing Feelings

I've learned some things about our conversations when we go out together. During those first few dates I had so much to talk about and was so pleased at rediscovering the pleasure of being alone with this beautiful woman who was so interested in *me,* that it was quite a while before I realized I was doing all the talking.

I would say, "Okay, Jennifer, tell me about your day," and she would sort of shrug and mumble, "Oh, you know, nothing happened." She had been taught, one way or another, that her time and her experiences were neither important nor interesting.

Gradually I learned to ask more specific questions: How did you feel when Nathan had a tantrum yesterday? How do you feel when he acts like that in public? How do you feel about our having the deacons over for supper? As she saw that I did think her thoughts and feelings were important, she learned to be open and share with me.

It may seem that our wives have benefitted the most from our clubtimes together, but that's not the case. I believe that we men gain the most. I need to take time for fun, too. I need to share thoughts with the one person in the world who cares most about me. And I've rediscovered the thrill and excitement of being with the most charming woman in the world—my wife! We FATHERS have grown to know and understand our sweethearts more deeply than ever before in our marriages.

The Big Little Things

Clubtime with Mommie doesn't always have to be a romantic date. Ordinary times spent together can be special when you make the effort to notice the little things that let her know she's special to you:

- Go shopping together and intentionally smile, showing an interest in the blouse she's looking at. Do not park yourself in the nearest chair while she shops (although that might be a first step in the right direction for some men).
- Know her sizes and favorite colors, what styles and fabrics she likes and dislikes.
- Notice that she has this "thing" for calico geese, teddy bears or gnomes. (One woman I know has little hippos all around the house; another has turtles.)

60

- Know her favorite foods and the best places to eat.
- Listen to her express her feelings.

Husbands and wives can learn to go shopping together, turning it into an opportunity to enjoy one another's company and get to know each other better. If a woman needs or enjoys extended shopping expeditions, I tell the FATHERS member to learn to go with her and hold his tongue. Any woman can appreciate that. The same is true for a wife who can learn to shop in places her husband enjoys—being patient, taking an interest and offering friendly suggestions. Jennifer and I no longer buy one another clothing without each other because it has become an activity we share.

Recently, while vacationing at a resort town, Jennifer and I were browsing at the showroom of a factory outlet that designs a particular type of casual skirt and cotton knit top. Because we were shopping at the factory, the clothes were discounted considerably. Jennifer tends to be cautious of overspending when shopping for clothes and she picked a skirt and a bright knit top that would match. I wanted her to pick out a second matching outfit because the style was different and because the price was reasonable. Jennifer did not want to buy a second set. She felt guilty about getting two. I found pleasure in wanting to provide something she would not have chosen. Our ability to communicate put us in touch with the feelings we had and helped us to then appreciate our differences. Incidentally, we left the store with two unique outfits!

As a way of showing that each couple is unique, FATHERS member Scott delights in surprising his wife each year with a new outfit on her birthday. It seems that Meg just loves surprises and that blesses them both. Their system works for them and our system works for us.

More Special Days

How can we give our wives pleasant surprises? What can be special this week? Can you stop by a card shop and pick out a "thinking of you" note to drop in the mail today? Can you buy just one daisy to lay on her pillow tonight? A number of these ideas come from other FATHERS members. Having a support group not only holds me accountable in giving weekly time to my wife, but it also generates my awareness of Jennifer and her particular needs.

One thing Jennifer hates to do is to put gas in the car. It was bad enough when the filling-station attendants would pump gas and wash the windows while she sat inside feeling foolish. But when the self-service pumps went in, Jennifer gave up. In her opinion, gas stations are hostile male territory and that's one area of liberation she'd rather do without.

On top of that, Jennifer worries about running out of gas and getting stuck. I'll put the car in neutral and coast down our hill, then wing it to work on a fume and a prayer. But not Jennifer. So I decided that I would bless her and take the responsibility to keep both of our cars filled up. Moreover, I decided not to say anything, so Jennifer would have the fun of discovering my blessing herself.

Well, one month went by, and then six weeks, and she still didn't notice and didn't say anything. I'd never have stuck it out without the FATHERS each week. They kept saying, "Hang in there. You have the joy of learning to serve. She'll notice eventually and that will be an extra blessing."

It was *three months* before Jennifer made any comment. She was so surprised and appreciative that I just bit my tongue and didn't even mutter, "Well, it's about time."

I remember a couple of birthday parties I had for Jennifer. These were not decade markers—30, 40, etc.—that we tend to celebrate in our society. I called several special friends and asked them to come over for a surprise party—minus the gifts. *They* would be the blessing. I had roses ready to place on her arm and a beauty-queen sash that said, "Most Loved, 1982." (The letters were written in glue on a wide ribbon, then sprinkled with glitter.) We had her sit in a chair in the center of the room and each guest told one thing about Jennifer that they appreciated— as well as a blessing that they would like to give her. For example, one friend said, "Jennifer always welcomes the neighborhood children—muddy feet, runny noses and all. So I'd like to bless her with a cookie jar that never gets empty."

Jennifer felt embarrassed in the beginning, but then she was uplifted, knowing that we all really noticed her, cared for her and appreciated her.

Blessing, Not Bungling

I want to caution you to choose a gift that will truly bless the one who receives it. One husband in FATHERS wanted to bless his wife after their second baby. He saved and sacrificed and bought her one full year's paid membership in Weight Watchers. Guess what? The gift didn't bless her one bit!

Be sensitive to your wife's needs, wants and personal desires. Don't give her what *you* want to have. Give her what *she* wants.

Here's a suggestion: Gather a week's worth of shirts, take them to be laundered and make that act a gift to your wife. You can give her a coupon which reads, "A gift to you this week, to give us more free time together. _____ shirts professionally laundered."

Also, when a child is small, consider ordering diaper service or having a cleaning lady come periodically, say once a month or every other month. If you are determined, you can find people who are willing to do this— even in small towns and communities. Sometimes high school students can be hired through a school counselor's office.

One of the things Jennifer enjoyed the most was a facial that I arranged for her to have in a downtown department store. That was one thing she had never wanted to spend the money for on herself. I made sure that her calendar was free, made the appointment and gave it to her as a gift.

Have you ever thought of surprising your wife by making arrangements to have her hair done? It's important for the wife working outside the home to have the confidence of looking her best in the work place where, unfortunately, women are still judged on their appearance. It's just as important for the wife working all day in the home to feel and look her best. First Corinthians 11:15 speaks of a woman's hair as being her glory and pride. Maybe there's a down-to-earth fact here that gets lost in the arguments over veils and headcoverings. The practical point I see is that a woman's hair is important to her. (As a minister I have noticed that when a woman is going into or coming out of surgery, nothing, not even prayer, perks her up like a really good hairdo.) The husband can recognize this truth to bless her.

Just Like Daddy

Dad can help his children learn to express appreciation and love to Mommy as he learns himself. Children will quickly pick up the practice of saying, "Great dinner,

Mom!" if Dad initiates the habit. Monkey see, monkey do can be a wonderful trait when what the "monkey" sees is Daddy putting out effort to show affection. For example, one FATHER collected a number of old magazines and spent a clubtime with his preschooler cutting out and gluing pictures to construction paper to make cards to give to Mommie during the week. For very young children, Dad can make simple dot-to-dot letters, letting the child connect the dots and spell their name and a message: "This is for you, Mama. I made it myself!"

There were also those interesting times when Jennifer was in the hospital for Nathan's or Christopher's births and I had the opportunity to see what it is like to be a single parent—what it means to prepare a meal when each of the kids wants something different and complains about what comes to the table. I learned what it's like to bathe them and to read them stories. I quickly learned that it isn't always easy. And then I learned that the same chores with one child become far more difficult with two—and then with three.

Because I had come to enjoy having more time with the children when Jennifer was in the hospital, I decided to continue taking responsibility for the children's bedtime ritual on evenings that I could be at home. I saw that my initiative not only gave Jennifer some time to do something she enjoys, it gave me extra time to be with each child individually *and* serve as a role model for the boys. Later on, my wife was relaxed and ready for some special time with me.

A Wife's Vacation

Jennifer had a particularly stressful time after Christopher was born. Her mother had died in November, just before his birth in December. The pain of grief continued for a long time and perhaps it was prolonged by the exhaustion of childbirth and caring for a new baby. Chrissy was 18 months old when it seemed right for Jennifer to visit her sister in Fargo, North Dakota.

When Jennifer settled in her seat on the airplane and looked around, she was suddenly aware of being alone. There was no little hand to hold or fingers to grab onto her dress, no worries about whether the baby would take a nap, no diaper bags, no meals or snacks to worry about. During those few days, Jennifer began to shut down her motors. She enjoyed sleeping soundly all night without getting up to feed the baby, being able to eat in restaurants, having somebody else prepare meals for her and all the other things some adults take for granted.

Jennifer needed that time away from the children. Being a homemaker and the mother of young children carries with it a unique combination of stress, servanthood, challenge and sometimes weariness.

Getting away from the responsibilities of home and children occasionally, whether it be for an hour, an afternoon or a few days isn't so much a prescription for escape and freedom as it is one of renewal and refreshment. She was only a phone call away and when I called, I gave detailed descriptions of the day's activities, of the night visitors I received crawling under my blankets, the fuzzy worms we found or the unbelievable thing a certain somebody had said.

After that first solo vacation I began to encourage Jennifer to get away at least once a year. So she began by going home to her family, to be "queen of leisure" for a couple of days in that setting. One year I sent her and a friend to a Christian seminar in Pittsburg where they stayed in the home of a church family. It was just a joy for her to be out, to travel and feel free. The next year she went with another friend to Shakertown, Kentucky. Upon her return she teased me a little, mentioning the Shakers' separation of males and females.

Jennifer's trips have evolved into a yearly time away from it all. And perhaps there is a kernel of truth in the Shaker separation, because every time we are apart, coming back together is so sweet!

Twenty-eight Days

Being sensitive to menstrual cycles has been very helpful in the FATHERS marriages. There is no mystery in menstruation, as the old-fashioned myth would have us believe. It is just a biological reality. The physical and emotional factors and varying degrees experienced by individual women in their menstrual cycle have prompted the current information on PMS—Premenstrual Syndrome.

Dr. James Dobson, in *What Wives Wish Husbands Knew About Women,* comments on the relationship of estrogen levels in the menstrual cycle and self-esteem. "Most important, she should interpret her feelings with caution and skepticism during her premenstrual period. If she can remember that the despair and sense of worthlessness are hormonally induced and have nothing to do with reality, she can withstand the psychological nosedive more easily."[1]

This is a time to be especially aware of your wife and her feelings. It may be that she cannot easily cope with her emotions and that for a few days she is not as rational as she would want to be—a frustrating situation.

The physical and psychological aspects of the monthly period is something husbands can and should understand. And while there's no need to pamper her, be especially sensitive. Even though you both know that her mood will soon change, it is wrong to discount or deny any irritation or anger. The feelings of the moment are very real. Assurance of your love (when she feels most unlovely), a hug, an unexpected love letter or a surprise can make all the difference in the world.

Not long ago, I realized Jennifer was feeling discouraged and overwhelmed before her menstrual cycle. She expressed her feelings of inability to cope with the boys' end-of-year schedules, feeling unappreciated by me and not being able to have any time to herself.

I knew that an evening with a friend would be a serendipity to her and communicate my sensitivity. She often takes the boys to movies *they* enjoy, but rarely sees one of her own choosing. I arranged for her friend Jan to pick her up. Jennifer was surprised when Jan appeared at the door with an invitation to see *Out of Africa*. Later that evening I saw the movie vicariously through her animated review.

It is the husband who thinks of his wife *first* that illustrates how to give yourself up as Christ loved the Church. I guarantee you, as the husband is mindful of his wife's welfare and feelings, she will begin to respond to him emotionally, to hear his own particular needs *and* to confide in him spiritually. As an openness in the spirit develops, she is open to him physically as well. There is a special blessing when two learn to become one in this special way.

The Greatest of These Is Love

Again, the key is an intentional, conscious decision to give up yourself and the things you want. We also have to give up feeling sorry for ourselves in order to be genuinely considerate of someone else's needs. And the most important someone else is your wife.

Each week, every man in FATHERS is called to account for his week: What have you done this week to make your wife feel special? Did you take her out? Did you give her a gift of words or of something material? Did you tell her how you feel when you see and touch her? If not, why?

These are the kinds of questions we must ask ourselves in this process of becoming better fathers and husbands and I confess that it is not always easy. But every time we think that we're sacrificing something for our wives, we inevitably discover that the rewards are far greater than the trivialities left behind.

> Love is very patient and kind, never jealous or envious, never boastful or proud, never haughty or selfish or rude. Love does not demand its own way. It is not irritable or touchy. It does not hold grudges and will hardly even notice when others do it wrong. It is never glad about injustice, but rejoices whenever truth wins out. If you love someone you will be loyal to him no matter what the cost. You will always believe in him, always expect the best of him, and always stand your ground in defending him.

> It's like this: when I was a child I spoke and thought and reasoned as a child does. But when I became a man my thoughts grew far beyond those of childhood, and now I have put away the childish things.

> There are three things that remain—faith, hope, and love—and the greatest of these is love (1 Cor. 13:4-7, 11, 13, *TLB*).

Tips

Surprise A.B.C. Time (the Affirmation Birthday Celebration). Add a special touch to those in-between milestone birthdays (ending in multiples of five) by secretly arranging with your wife's friends or neighbors to come to your home for a surprise birthday celebration. Inform each to think of one or two Christian character qualities that your wife reminds her of. These qualities will be communicated verbally to your wife and may be done so through some object such as a flower, vase, picture, pin, etc. These little mementos will be treasures to your wife. Select a date when she will be home, station yourself near the door to receive your invited guests, slip out after having surprised her and serve whatever refreshments you have arranged.

Surprise Birthday or Special-Day Calls. Prearrange by letter or phone for friends and relatives to call your wife on special occasions. Oftentimes this can also be done on those not-so-special times, too, and suddenly transform them into special occasions. Offer to those calling long distance to pay for the call by having them call collect.

The Shopping Spree. Select some dates on your calendar to go shopping with your wife. Although these dates should occur before family events such as holidays, birthdays and special occasions, also select some "ordinary" times just to be together—to browse and window-shop. When you shop, challenge yourself to be a participant with her rather than a spectator. Accept the challenge of not sitting down on the chairs in the dress shops. Tell her you want her to look for something in your favorite color and allow her to model for you.

Family Secret Service Projects. Gather your children together and form a secret service organization. Younger children love it! Ask each child to select some service projects he/she can do for Mom that will be done in secret and be a blessing to her. These projects can be done over a week's duration. Make a game of it to see when Mom notices and comments on what is "mysteriously" being done. Whose project will Mom notice first? Prearrange a family secret code to be communicated when she notices, like a wink or smile at one another. When she has finally noticed all the projects, inform her of the secret service club and caution her to be careful because she may come across some future actions from the club!

Honey Do List. Consider taking the initiative to walk about your home, room to room, corner to corner, and make up a "do" list. Sit your wife down (so that she doesn't faint) and inform her of your "honey do" list and allow her to select the projects she desires most to be done. Your initiative will be greatly appreciated and probably shocking. Then, of course, set about doing the projects for your honey!

Rocking Your Babies to Sleep. Discuss with your wife the possibility of buying a rocking chair for the purpose of your rocking the children before they go to bed. She may think that you are "off your rocker," but inform her that you would like for her to have some personal time for herself away from your children on certain evenings. Begin to take your children and rock them while reading or singing to/with them in preparation for their sleep. *Everyone* will be blessed!

TAKING INVENTORY

1. How many of the following can you identify concerning your wife:
   a. Her feelings concerning her time involvement with the family.
   b. Her dreams and aspirations.
   c. Her areas of personal pride and success.
   d. Her greatest source of joy.
   e. Her greatest source of stress.
   f. Her greatest irritation.

2. List on paper five things about which you can compliment your wife. Circle those you have told her about in the last week.

3. The Scriptures call husbands to love their wives by sacrificing themselves. What is your definition of "sacrificial love"? Compare it with your wife's. In what specific ways are you growing in sacrificial love?

4. What are some activities or interests that your wife pursued prior to marriage and family obligations? Does she have opportunity for these now? Who are her closest friends? How often are they together? What could you specifically do to encourage these activities?

5. How do you feel about giving your wife a night off and out? Do you look at it as a gift, a necessity, or a regular practice? What would she do if nobody bothered her for an evening?

6. When is the last time you kept the children so your wife could spend time with an adult friend or pursue personal interests? Discuss with your wife what she would

like to have extended time for away from home and child care responsibilities in order for her to accomplish this desire.

7. Do you ever take responsibility for preparation of meals, doing laundry or shopping for your wife?

Chapter 5

Taking Time to Be with Your Family

Husbands, love your wives, as Christ loved the church and gave himself up for her (Eph. 5:25).

Greater love has no man than this, that a man lay down his life for his friends (John 15:13).

It isn't difficult to recognize in these verses the concept of giving up what is ours to bless others—especially, but not only, for our wives. The Ephesians passage echoes John 15:13, where it is clear that the way Christians are to love is by giving up themselves.

Think about this for a moment. We hear these verses so often, but do we understand what this means in practical, day-to-day relationships? The way Christians are to love is by giving up time, energy and resources from our own needs and wants for the sake of another person's needs and wants. Take Time Day reminds us to give up time from our daily working schedule to be with our family members.

Have We Met Somewhere? At Home?

When Jennifer and I were both students at the University of North Dakota from 1962 to 1963, we saw each other every day. Then I went to graduate school and we were together every weekend. But I transferred to McCormick Theological Seminary and the next year we saw one another only on holidays. It occurred to me that our relationship was going in the wrong direction: every day to every weekend, and then every holiday. But absence makes the heart grow fonder and after four years of dating, we were married. We *thought* that we'd return to being together every day. Ha!

That was when I took that first church in Minnesota. I saw good results from hard work and my efforts to live out Ecclesiastes 3:22: "So I saw that there is nothing better than that a man should enjoy his work, for that is his lot . . . . " During this time Jennifer was teaching and we were both happy and satisfied with our jobs. But something was missing. I was ignoring Ecclesiastes 4:6: "Better is a handful of quietness than two hands full of toil and a striving after wind." You see, I never took a day off!

One day my parents came to visit and I agreed to stay home because it was important to Jennifer to have a day together with just the family. I decided that the best way to use my time was to be down in the basement, working in my workshop. Before long Dad joined me, fiddling around with the tools and gently steering our conversation toward my schedule. He wasn't pushy; he was gentle. After awhile he went back upstairs and Mom came down.

76

Same thing. She didn't scold, but politely suggested that maybe I might be working a little hard. She went back up to the kitchen and pretty soon Jennifer came down. "Ron, couldn't you put that down for just a little while?"

One after another, they were trying to get through to me: I was a workaholic and needed to change my ingrained habits.

We moved to Cincinnati when our first son was a year old. The house wasn't completely finished and we hurried to fix up the first floor where we planned to invite prayer and fellowship groups. Within six weeks we had 120 guests in our home—which looked just fine as long as you didn't go upstairs or downstairs. But that was where Jennifer and Joshua were living—on the unfinished second floor and in the basement!

I wish I could say that things changed quickly, but I can't. Jennifer kept in touch with my life by sharing in the ministry until the second baby was born. Then things began to change for her.

Although we still invited church members to our home on Sunday afternoons, it didn't seem to be working as well. Jennifer used to enjoy inviting folks over, but now she wasn't very enthusiastic. What was wrong with this woman? And there were the "special" things we couldn't do anymore. We couldn't go camping together by ourselves or run out for a late-night pizza or drop in on friends. Anytime I wanted to do something, Jennifer would have to haul along a carload of diapers, bottles, toys and equipment. Other times she'd just sigh and say she'd rather stay home. It seemed that all the romantic, fun times were gone. She was always busy nursing the newborn and chasing the toddler and for some reason she seemed to be tired all the time. Obviously, Jennifer had a problem.

No! The problem was my enormous insensitivity, my failure to recognize her need for rest and attention and my lack of participation with the children.

Do you see what had happened? Early in our relationship I had allowed my priorities to fall out of balance. How could I give my love to Jennifer when I was unwilling to give my time to her? It took me a long time to realize that just as daily time with the Lord is vital to the life of a Christian, meaningful time together is essential to the life of a marriage.

The Challenge of Being the Host

> The Spirit and the Bride say, "Come." And let him who hears say, "Come." And let him who is thirsty come, let him who desires take the water of life without price (Rev. 22:17).

It is the nature of Christ to be the host. The nature of the host is to consider the needs of the guest and to make arrangements for his/her comfort. He sets aside time to plan for all the little details that will bring the guest pleasure. The husband is to serve the wife this way and the wife is to serve the husband this way—both appealing to the Christian nature within them through grace. We are to serve the needs of our spouse by thinking of him/her as the guest.

How would you treat a weekend guest? If your sweetheart lived a thousand miles away, and you only had one weekend to spend together, how would you treat her? Would you make her bed with fresh linens and set out your best towels and new bars of soap? Would you have her favorite ice cream in the freezer? Would you greet her with flowers? Would you go out for breakfast on Sunday morning and sit with your arm around her in church? Would you linger late over another cup of coffee and hang on every word she said? Or would you read the sports page while she did the dishes?

A couple of years back, Jennifer was planning a celebration for my birthday and she wanted very much for the whole thing to be a surprise. So she set aside a little money each week and she carefully planned an evening together. She checked my schedule with my secretary, chose a restaurant, made reservations and arranged baby-sitting. That was a big undertaking for her, because it is more her nature to just go along with plans made by other people. But Jennifer was determined to carry everything through and she did, right up to picking up the bill at the restaurant and announcing to the waiter, "The gentleman is *my* guest this evening!"

Another wife wanted to do something special for her husband's birthday, but their budget was too tight for any kind of evening out. So the day before his birthday she called as many of his friends as she could reach and asked them to phone him at work the next day to sing, "Happy Birthday." Not only did he receive phone calls all day long, but several of his bolder buddies dropped in and sang their wishes in person! He was celebrated and blessed all day long, for no more expense than time and thoughtfulness.

Meeting the needs of one another also applies to taking time for one another. How do extra-marital affairs begin? I believe that the seeds of trouble are planted when a woman has not been treated as a guest by her spouse— she has not been made to feel welcome, special, appreciated or celebrated. Then someone else comes into the picture and offers to be host. It feels so good to be treated like a star! It's great to be admired and fussed over! And oh, to be recognized and hosted by someone who cares about my needs and my pleasures! Is it any wonder that the temptation becomes irresistible? If only husbands and wives would be more sensitive, understanding, creative and generous to one another. If only they'd be less accusing and less blaming in sexual relationships!

Of course, it is easier to host a guest who really is only a temporary visitor. We can ignore their warts and idiosyncrasies if we know that they will be gone by Monday. The real challenge is to be gracious to the one who is staying permanently. That's when we realize that we can't love like this with our own abilities. You have to let Christ flow through you, for He is the One who came to be the host in serving others. He will be the host to your family, through you.

Take Time to Be with Your Family

I read words to the song *Cat's in the Cradle* in my Father's Day sermon in 1981 and my own feelings of inadequacy and guilt were so strong that I broke down and wept in the pulpit. The congregation wept with me. We were all guilty, every one of us. Our lives are much like the road to hell; they are paved with good intentions. We are in danger of coming to the end of our lives and looking back on wasted years, our memories tainted with broken promises and late-great expectations.

It isn't easy for a father to find the time to be with his wife and each child every week. For some of us, finding time for the kids seems like a hopeless proposition. After all, what do you do when you have an appointment with an important client at work? You write it into your schedule and make it a priority. Does it seem silly to schedule appointments with your children? Believe me, there is no client more important or deserving of your time than your child. Your client could go to another business man to get his work done, but there is *no other man* your child can turn to for a father's love!

"Men do not instinctively know how to be loving husbands and caring fathers," observed one of my wife's friends. "The FATHERS Ministry is tremendous because it helps meet a natural void in men. Men must be taught *how!*"

Just as it is necessary to commit time to your wife in order to have a healthy relationship with her, it is also necessary to commit time to each of your children. Remember, these precious kids will only be young for a short while. You have a *kairos* amount of time to nurture and to teach them in the ways of the Lord; a limited amount of time to give them the father's love that they need.

F.A.T.

In his book, *What Wives Wish Their Husbands Knew About Women,* James Dobson comments on the cliché, "Well, it's more important to give our children quality time than quantity." His comment is set in a discussion about working mothers:

> Who says that a working mother's evening time with her children is necessarily of greater quality than it would have been if she remained at home all day? Her fatigue would make the opposite more likely. Anyway, why must we choose between these desirable components: let's give our babies both quality *and* quantity.[1]

Amen! Dads, are you listening? As one of our FATHERS members points out, it is absolutely necessary to have quantity time for quality time to happen! Anyone who gives 5 or 10 minutes a day to his kids is kidding himself if he thinks that is quality time.

> Why do you spend your money for that which is not bread, and your labor for that which does not satisfy? Hearken diligently to me, and eat what is good, and delight yourselves in *fat*ness! (Isa. 55:2, italics added).

F.A.T. stands for Focused Attention Time. Remember my habit of leaving the concerns of work aside before coming into the home? Your children need your 100 percent attention, your focused attention. When you talk with your child, look into his/her eyes and listen to the meaning he/she is trying to convey with those childish words.

In Dr. Ross Campbell's book, *How to Really Love Your Child,* three ways to communicate love are described: by eye contact, by physical contact and by focused attention. Remembering to maintain eye contact when the child is speaking and touching the child often (with pats, a hand on the shoulder, a gentle nudge or a playful punch) are all ways of filling up that child's emotional "gas tank." These are ways beyond mere speech that say, "You are here and I am with you."

We Teach Theology in the Family

> Remember also your Creator in the days of your youth (Eccles. 12:1).

A denominational study reveals that if Dad and Mom *both* attend church regularly, 72 percent of their children remain faithful. If only *Mom* attends church regularly, 15

82

percent remain faithful. But if only *Dad* attends regularly, 55 percent remain faithful. This example of the father's role is critical as a model of faith. If we want our children to remember God in their youth, it is our responsibility as fathers to give them the time and experiences by which they *will* remember God. It is up to us to create and fill their memory banks with experiences they will draw upon throughout their lives. The memories won't be there unless we create them, now.

My father, who is now 75, was an obstetrician in our little town in North Dakota. He was often out delivering babies in the wee hours of the morning. I remember seeing my father every morning with his Bible and a daily devotional. He never had to explain it, but I saw that in spite of a lack of sleep and the burden of the day ahead, time with God was important to him. His disciplined faith has been a model for me throughout my life.

My maternal grandparents also modeled a strong family faith. They were simple people who spent their lives at the farm. My sister and I visited often and we slept upstairs where it was very cold in the winter. In the mornings we hurried down to the kitchen to dress beside the warm wood stove, while Grandfather had his coffee. He would pour cream into the coffee, pour the coffee into the saucer to cool it, then pour it back into the cup. As a small boy, I thought this was a fascinating ritual.

Grandfather began every morning by reading the Bible in Czech, even though Grandmother would scold him, saying, "Read in English when Ruthie and Ronnie are here!"

Grandfather would always answer, "Ruthie and Ronnie need to learn to respect God's Word whether they can understand it or not."

Grandmother, who lived to be 98, never prayed out loud that I can recall. But I remember going into her room to kiss her goodnight and finding her on her knees in prayer. When she realized I was in the room she would say, "Just a minute, Ronnie, I'll be with you in a moment." In that way, I learned that prayer was to be respected and not interrupted.

When we went to church I remember sitting in oak pews high off the floor and swinging my legs to the organ music. I might kick the pew ahead of me and Grandfather would apply a "laying on of hands," shaping his mouth into a silent, *"No!"*

Now, so many years away from those times, I realize that the Lord laid in store a marvelous treasure for my sister and me in the parents and grandparents we shared. The theology—the understanding of God's presence in our lives—they gave us far exceeds anything I learned in seminary.

Clubtime

When Nathan was four, I was spending quite a bit of time with seven-year-old Joshua in little League Ball games and in Cub Scouts. It was Joshua who noticed that there was something unfair in this and he came up with an idea.

"Dad," he said, "why don't you and Nathan start your own club? He's too little for Scouts, but you could do the same kind of stuff with just him."

What wisdom from a child! I talked to Nathan and he decided we should start the "Batman Club." During our first clubtime we drove out to a fabric store and he chose gray material and Batman appliques. Jennifer then stitched up two neckerchiefs like those worn in Scouts and we made up a secret password and a secret handshake (I can't tell you what they were—they're secret!) Every Thursday evening at 7:00 we had clubtime and our activities were determined entirely by Nathan: sometimes we spent an hour in his room playing with building blocks. Other times we went to the park for an expedition in the woods or to the mall to have a soft drink and check out the new models in the toy shop.

Clubtime is now a basic principle in the FATHERS Ministry and each dad is committed to spend one hour of Focused Attention Time with each child, every week. Of course, sometimes clubtime has to be rescheduled or shortened because of a pressing circumstance. But when a child knows that he or she is important to Dad, and can see his or her own name written in Dad's appointment book, it's wonderful how flexible and forgiving that child can be. Kids are sensitive and know when it's a "catch as catch can" time and when it's a carefully scheduled priority time.

I remember not too long ago, when I was having my prayer time, the boys were awake earlier than usual because it was Saturday morning. Nathan came bouncing into my office asking something about cartoons on television and I very gently (I hope) said something about not disturbing me, please, while I was talking to our heavenly Father. So Nathan left but a few minutes later there was a rattle at the door. I heard Nathan saying to his little brother, "No, no, Chrissy, don't bother Daddy now. He and God are having clubtime together!"

Clubtime Rules

During some weeks there may only be 15 minutes for clubtime, but if you are there and giving 100 percent, it can be enough. (There are some tips at the end of this chapter for things to do in only 15 minutes.) With the buddy and squad leader to keep each FATHERS member accountable, there are fewer shortened times and more hours spent with our children. The emphasis is on commitment.

These are the rules for clubtime:

1. Spend clubtime with a particular child *alone.* No other child may join in. If you are in a room, no other child may come in. If you go to the zoo or make some other trip for clubtime, go alone.

2. Do what the child chooses to do, for this is not a time for Dad's favorite game or pastime. Neither is it a time for an activity that makes Dad look good. It's time to let the child be in charge.

One week Nathan decided that we should go to the local discount store to do some shopping. So we got there and I lifted him into the shopping cart.

"Va-room! Here's the super Batmobile shooting out of the Batcave!" We zipped down the center aisle. "There goes the Joker. Let's go get him!" We careened around the hardware counter. "And Batman and Robin have the desperate criminal cornered!" The Batmobile screeched to a sudden halt.

Standing directly in front of us was a matron of our church, Mrs. Dignity herself.

"Well! Hello, *Doctor* Rand?"

"Oh, uh, hello, Mrs. Dignity, how nice to see you." I swallowed and tried to grin. "You know my son, Nathan, don't you?"   .

Nathan popped up from the shopping cart. "Hi! It's clubtime, so we can't talk now. C'mon, Dad, let's find the Hot Wheels!" Humility is a beautiful gift from God.

Other wonderful times more than make up for the occasional embarrassments. Chris's inevitable choice for clubtime always had something to do with trains and we received special permission to visit the Chessie System rail yard to watch the trains. We would wear railroaders' hats and put a blanket on the hood of the car and sit watching the diesels switch cars and tracks. Through our repeated visits we came to know a friendly engineer who let Chris get up into the cab with him and "drive" the train.

Camp Outs

Another special thing many FATHERS members do during clubtime is go on a "camp out." After the evening meal, announce to the family that you and a selected child are going camping. Then go to be alone in a room with that child and allow no one to interfere. Shutting the door is allowed, if necessary, to exclude pestering siblings (with the assurance that they will have their own camp out according to the schedule). You can then spend as much time as possible with that child reading books, rubbing backs, being silly, telling stories, praying, etc. Stay with that child until he or she is asleep. Next, go and have a camp out with Mommy.

At times some fathers like to take sleeping bags and lay on the floor together, falling asleep *that* way. If you want, you may slip back in the morning and wake up with that child. The important time to be there is from supper time until your child falls asleep.

Let the older children, especially girls, get into their pajamas privately. Then rub their backs, talk, play cards or whatever, leaving after they fall asleep. The idea is to do the same things you would do if you were camping in a tent for the night.

In-charge Time

Another practice growing out of clubtime is "In-charge Time." This is a day designated for a particular child to be "in charge," indicating both responsibility and privilege. The child "in charge" is responsible for setting the table for the meals that day, perhaps planning and helping to prepare the meals, reading the Bible verses, saying the blessing, clearing the table, doing the dishes and any other household duties. The privileges include sharing the good things of the day first, being served food first, having the first selection of TV, having the first time with a parent and so forth. Families with several children can alternate days of the week, with the parents "in charge" on Sunday.

Traveling Companions

As children mature, clubtime can also extend to trips. Many fathers have experimented with great success with the idea of taking a child with them on business trips to other cities and countries where their work takes them. It means making extra arrangements and takes some careful planning, but the benefits make the effort so worthwhile!

For example, I frequently fly into a city and hold two-or-three-day evangelism clinics. I normally stay with a family of the sponsoring church, so I will ask the person making the clinic arrangements to place me with a family who has children my son's age. I explain that my son will assist me at the clinic the first evening, but would like to tag along with the family to music lessons, shopping, ball games or whatever they normally do on Saturdays.

I can't remember any clinic where this caused difficulty and the benefits for the boys have been enormous. We have the pleasure of traveling together, experiencing airline procedures and meals and meeting schedules. We see new cities and experience all the flavor and excitement of different regions. We get to know many different families and observe how Christians are considerate and caring wherever we go.

When I took Christopher to St. Louis, he stayed with a

family that went to the zoo on Saturday and ate at McDonalds. Before the host family opened the burgers and fries they all bowed their heads and prayed. Later they read Bible stories before bedtime. It was so good for Chris to see that it's not just his dad who prays at restaurants or reads the Bible—other Christian families, all over the world, do these same things.

Other FATHERS members have also found that it is possible to take a child on business trips. Most often they stay with friends or acquaintances or sleep in hotels, and have a friend welcome their child only while the business obligations are being taken care of. Then they have lunchtimes or evenings free to explore a new city together. Once FATHERS recognized the possibilities of taking children on trips, more and more men are discovering that it is worthwhile to make arrangements and work it out together.

Surprisingly, the father discovers that he enjoys the trip more himself when a child is along. I used to book a flight into a city with barely enough time to make it to my appointment and rush back home on the earliest plane. Friends would ask, "How was Portland?" and I'd have to say, "I don't know. I only saw the inside of one church!" Now, with Joshua, Nathan or Christopher along, I arrive early enough to visit with our hosts, schedule time to see the sights of the area and maybe even stay over an extra night so we won't be rushed.

We learn things about our children on these trips together that somehow we overlook at home. I was in Taipei with Joshua at a missionary complex and during one of the conference sessions there was an opportunity for missionary children to stay with baby-sitters so that both parents could be free for a little while. Joshua saw this as an area where he could serve, so he volunteered to help take care of some children. I was able to observe him and it was wonderful to see how his gifts of creativity came out. How he would create games and play! I realized that he has a real gift of dealing with small children.

Another time I was with Nathan at a FATHERS Ministry clinic in South Africa. In a question-and-answer period following one of the seminars, most of the questions were directed toward Nathan. There seemed to be some confusion about clubtime so Nathan said, "My dad will do whatever I want to do for clubtime. Like if I want to go out for tea, he will take me out for tea . . . . " He went on to explain.

Well, I could hardly wait until that session was over to grab Nathan and hug him. I said, "Do you realize what you did, Nathan? We've never gone out for tea—in fact, you don't even like tea! Yet you were sensitive to the Holy Spirit who led you to use an illustration that really communicated to your listeners. Way to go, Son!"

I was so proud, I nearly popped the buttons off my shirt!

Choosing to Take the Time

We need to be with our wives and children the way our heavenly Father chooses to be with us. God the Father does not just yell down from heaven, "I love you." He does not say, "Here's the answer to your prayer, now run along and have a good time." God the Father chose to be *with* us 100 percent of the time. The Son also chooses to be with us, to listen and really hear what we are saying and to give us quality and quantity time. And beyond that, He sends His Holy Spirit to be with us 100 percent. If the great God of all the universe can take that kind of time to be with the ones He loves, how can we say we are too busy to do the same?

Tips

Here are a number of short-order clubtimes the FATHERS Ministry has developed:

The Motorcyle. Take your child on your lap. Your thumbs are the handle grips, your feet (if he/she can reach them) are the pedals. Your child kicks the throttle, you make motor noises and off you both go! Tip back and forth, rare up and backwards to "pop a wheelie," squeal around curves, jump over a ditch and crash in a heap onto the floor.

Visit the Zoo. Your child climbs on your back and names the animal he/she wants you to be.

The Elephant. Lumber in heavy steps, swaying side to side. Swing one arm as a trunk and reach up overhead several times to "trumpet."

The Alligator. Crawl on your belly on the floor.

The Boa Constrictor. Wriggle on the floor at first. Then suddenly twist around and give your child a big squeeze!

The Kangaroo. Hop around the room until exhausted.

Big-time Wrestling. Wrestle in a room where there aren't a lot of breakables. Think of any object that comes to your mind and say, "I talked with my friend Joe yesterday and he showed me the 'telephone' hold. His son is 13 and can't get out of this hold." Then wrestle around and get your child in a tight hold, but let him/her work lose without *too* much difficulty. Then say, "Wow, you're really good! Joe's 13-year-old couldn't get out of that hold, but you got out in about 29 seconds!"

Whenever I'm out of town, I use it as an occasion to introduce a new hold: "This is the St. Louis hold and you'll never get out of this one! The big kids there put this on one another and they can't get loose . . . . "

Remember to assure your child that a child older and stronger cannot break out of this hold. That always makes your child feel really super.

The Washing Machine. Sit on the floor with your child stretched over your lap. "My, my, you need to be washed," you say. "We'll have to . . .

- Pour in the water (tickle) and add a little soap (tickle).
- Now turn on the washer (shake up and down and around.)
- Use some fabric softener (tickle).
- Now rinse (tickle and shake).
- Next we spin dry (stand up and spin your child around) and hang you up to dry (hold your child upside down, if possible).
- Now we iron (stretch him/her out on the couch and "iron") and fold you up (fold up arms and legs).
- Finally we put you in the drawer (plop him/her onto another chair or couch)."

To make clubtimes special, remember that surprises bring pleasure in proportion to how out of the ordinary the activities are.

TAKING INVENTORY

1. Think of each of your children as being five years older than they are now. Name two specific things that you would like to have accomplished with each one by then.

What might you need to consider now for these things to happen?

2. Think five years ahead in your marriage. Discuss two or three specific things that you would like to develop over those years. How do you see these things being accomplished? What will be your part?

3. Describe your routine at home from the moment you arrive from work until you go to bed. If building individual relationships with each family member is important, what changes in your daily routine must you make to accomplish this goal? What changes must you make in your weekend routine as well?

4. How many of the following can you name about your children: their favorite foods, best friends or playmates, school or Sunday School teachers, things that excite or interest them most, favorite music groups and songs?

5. (a) How much time have you given your children in the past two weeks? (b) How often do you attend something your children take part in, such as athletic practice, scouting, music lessons? (c) When was the last time you wrestled with or had physical time with your children? (d) What one thing will you do in the next week to improve the time you spend with each one?

6. What treats or special things can you provide or do for your children or wife that will let them know they are special and loved? Name some specifically. What could you do this week that would be a treat for your family?

7. Do you ever plan special events or field trips that your family enjoys? What could you do in the near future to facilitate this?

Chapter 6

Inventive Family Worship

Ever be filled and stimulated with the [Holy] Spirit (Eph. 5:18, AMP).

A Middle Eastern papyrus was found recently named the Gospel of Thomas. Apparently a collection of Jesus' sayings, some are the same as those recorded in Matthew, Mark and Luke, but some are different. One of these sayings goes like this:

> Jesus said, "The Kingdom of the Father is like a certain woman who was carrying a jar full of meal. While she was walking on a road, still some distance from home, the handle of the jar broke and the meal emptied out behind her on the road. She did not realize it; she had noticed no accident. When she reached her house, she set the jar down and found it empty."[1]

Are we like that woman? Are we letting the Kingdom of God slip through our fingers without noticing? The time we have to love our spouses and to instruct our children is gradually sifting away while our minds are on other things. We are losing irreplaceable sustenance: the Kingdom of God!

Regular Times, Special Times

Usually our family takes time to worship together around the breakfast and supper tables. If we can possibly be together for a morning meal, we pray before we eat as a blessing. Afterwards we have a time of thanksgiving and pray for each family member for the coming day. Many mornings are rushed and we just can't sit down for a quality time together (Sundays are the most hectic in our home), but we worship in the mornings whenever we can.

Evening meals together are more regular and that's when we count on having regular worship together. When the schedule is full, we try to have a simpler meal so time is used in fellowship rather than in elaborate food preparation and cleanup. Whichever child is "in charge" for the day says the blessing before we eat and reads a passage of Scripture after we are finished.

A FATHERS member reported a time when his son Tommy was reading 1 Kings 18:27 (they use *The Living Bible*, a paraphrase Ken Taylor wrote to communicate better with his own children). It is the story of Elijah and the prophets of Baal and verse 27 reads, "'You'll have to shout louder than that,' he scoffed, 'to catch the attention of your god! Perhaps he is talking to someone, or is out sitting on the toilet . . . !'"

"What?" Dad interrupted. "Tommy, it doesn't say that!"

"But Dad, it says that right here: 'out sitting on the toilet!'"

They all looked and indeed, *The Living Bible* gives a very blunt rendering of the Hebrew mockery of Baal. That entire family got the giggles and had a delightful lesson on God's sense of humor.

Should you continue this practice when having friends and guests for dinner? Absolutely! I firmly believe that part of our responsibility as fathers is to model family worship for other families. When my family gets together in our home to celebrate and have a good time, we make certain that worshiping together is part of that celebration. Again, it may only be a few minutes, but it is there. And I have urged the members of our congregation to do the same in their homes.

Give Your *All* to Worship

How many times have we sought in family worship to have a special time and it just didn't happen? It just doesn't work when we say, "Com'on you kids, sit down and shut up. We're gonna worship now!"

To avoid unpleasant worship experiences such as this, we need to be aware that we are made up of four basic parts and these parts need to be in harmony in order to worship.

Mind

Worship is a learned expression. We don't know naturally how to worship God, so we learn acceptable denominational forms of worship. Those of us who grew up in white Presbyterian churches learn a different form of worship than those of us who are raised in black Pentecostal or Hispanic Catholic churches. No form of worship is right or wrong, only different.

Emotions

Worship is also a subjective experience. The emotions, for example, are often controlled by those worshipers involved in conservative denominations. And while weeping in worship may be discouraged, *other* traditions *encourage* crying or laughing out loud.

Body

Worship is an objective experience. One can worship as an act of obedience without "feeling" the presence of God (see Rom. 12:1). I believe there is value in participating in a worship service purely out of obedience to God.

Spirit

We are spiritual beings. Something must transpire as we are touched by the Spirit of God and as we give permission to the Spirit to move within us to prompt worship.

I should admit that there are times when we don't feel like worshiping. I remember one time when I came home following a very difficult week. I was exhausted from serving other people. I felt that I had given out so much loving to others and was receiving very little in return. Jennifer was busy throughout the meal with the boys and no one was paying much attention to me.

At the end of supper, when we turned to our Bible passage, I read a verse that had to do with love. I was really having a pity party by then, feeling nobody loved me. Nathan, who was about two and a half at the time, seemed to understand the moment and my feelings. He got down from his stool, climbed up on my lap, put his grubby little hands around my neck and with his bib against my cheeks (and most of his meal on the bib) said, "I lub bu, Daddy. I lub bu, I lub bu!"

That absolutely melted me and caused me to see that even when I felt unloved, I was loved. God used the family to make that love visible.

Personality Types and Styles of Worship

In family worship, flexibility is the key. I can't emphasize this fact too often. The goal of family worship is to build into the child the basic attitude and knowledge that God is present and available, active and concerned in every element of his/her life. Any style of worship that leads toward this goal is acceptable. Any form of worship that tends to block that goal—making God appear distant, irrelevant, boring or unpleasant—is unacceptable.

Personality types influence our family worship just as they affect our style of prayer. *SJ* types prefer orderly, regular, specific worship—as when a series of selected Bible verses is read each day, followed by a specific form of prayer (the Lord's Prayer, perhaps) and a hymn. They might even like to follow the liturgical calendar.

On the other hand, *FP*s probably prefer to worship spontaneously each day, depending on their personal circumstances, mood, etc. They might like to spend one entire day singing worship songs and the next day reading a long passage from the Psalms, an Epistle or some appropriate children's book. They may even want to march around the table singing "Onward Christian Soldiers."

Never allow family worship to be dreary! Be imaginative! Songs, silence, study or drama can all be expressions of your worship. You might act out one of the parables, with various member portraying the various characters. (Watch out for too much enthusiasm on the part of the robbers in the story of the Good Samaritan. We don't want to be so "spiritual" that someone comes to bodily harm!)

It's not likely that every member in any family will have the same preferences, so it's important to either experiment until you find a style that is meaningful to everyone or be willing to use different styles from time to time.

We've found it very helpful, when children are young, to light a candle during prayer—especially during seasons when it is beginning to be dark at suppertime. It is also good to light a candle when praying in their rooms at bedtime. It makes the point that God is present not only at the supper table, but also in their rooms. This can be enhanced with a night-light in the form of a praying child or a white cross. We have used these visual aids as a reminder that Jesus is the light of the world, watching over us in the time of darkness.

FATHERS member Jim says that in addition to daily bedtime prayers, once a week he and his wife lay hands on and pray for each child, making certain to pray for individual experiences and needs. It makes for some pretty silly prayers sometimes as the girls are three and five and they often pray for dolls and wooly worms, but those are the things that are important to the children. And they love it. It seems to mean so much to them that Mommy and Daddy will actually take time to lay on hands and pray for them specifically. And Jim is amazed that the girls insisted from the very beginning that they be allowed to lay hands on Mommy and Daddy and pray for them in the same way.

Setting Goals for Spiritual Growth

Some of us do better when we are working with a detailed plan or framework to reach specific goals. FATHERS member Bob and his wife Carol have developed a set of five goals that they keep in mind and their system has served as a model for other families in the FATHERS

100

Ministry. They use the five fingers of the hand to organize their goals.

Thumb: Time with the Lord

At one time Bob and Carol had family devotions together with their children and they all studied the same passage and prayed together, etc. But more recently each member is working on his/her own passage and having individual time with the Lord. They are together, but worshiping separately. This works well for Bob's family at this time.

Index Finger: Involved with Others

Carol knows it is important for their children to learn that discipleship means reaching out to others, so they invite international students from the local university to celebrate holidays with their family. Some of these students become close friends and are then invited to share the everyday times, to be a part of their lives and to be involved with others in a meaningful way.

Middle Finger: Memorization of Scripture

Hiding the Word in the heart allows the Spirit to bring that Word to bear in every situation of every day. There are several good programs and systems that families might use.[2]

Ring Finger: Relationships

Because Bob and Carol want their children to know how to keep relationships right and healthy, this family makes the effort to learn how to be angry without wounding each other, how to really listen to each other and how to ask for forgiveness when they fail. Bob and Carol have taken advantage of the many adult classes offered at our church and have passed this knowledge on to their children through practicing it at home every day.

Little Finger: Leading Others to Christ

Again, this family has taken advantage of the evangelism training offered at church and teach their children to be aware of daily opportunities to introduce their friends to Christ using their lips and their lives.

What are your goals to develop your family's spirituality through the opportunities that present themselves every day? Although your plan may not be as specific as Bob and Carol's, nevertheless I believe every couple should have at least one or two goals to pass on to their children and to following generations in the development of their own spirituality.

Logs and Splinters

An important part of our worshiping together is being able to confess our faults to one another. Confession keeps the channels of love between us clear of the splinters and the logs that can pile up into a tremendous logjam. We can't be close to each other if there's a logjam of resentments between us. If I'm holding onto my own grudges and my own need to be right and to show Jennifer that she's wrong, there's no way that we can have a close relationship. We can't be filled with the Holy Spirit and the joy of the Lord when we've clogged our spirits with logs.

The only way to clear the channel of logs is confession. I may see what *Jennifer* is doing wrong—that's the "splinter." But it's harder for me to see what *I'm* doing wrong—that's the "log" that's causing the jam. It's a basic principle in psychology that when I am irritated at somebody, it's probably because I have that same fault myself. I might be consciously unaware of my own fault or I might be unwilling to admit it. Either way, that's my log. When I own up to my own fault I can confess it and get rid of it by being forgiven. Only then does the logjam start to break up. Love and communication can flow between us again and God can use us as channels of His Spirit to one another.

It's even harder to clear out the logs between myself and the boys. My wife already knows that I'm not perfect, but I really want my kids to think I'm great. I mean, I'm their dad and they ought to look up to me. Right? Wrong. Face it, the kids are going to find out sooner or later that the old man's human. I might as well admit it straight out, and avoid being dishonest with them.

It had been two long days and I hadn't eaten anything but clear liquids due to a bout with stomach trouble. Jennifer had served a beautiful and fragrant meal and I was doing the dishes, even though I didn't eat. As I stood at the sink washing dishes with Nathan, who was being teased by Joshua over something or other, I blew up like a firecracker, accusing Joshua of lying to Nathan. Well, when you call your son a liar, you cut him to the quick, and he went down into the basement crying.

After we finished the dishes, Nathan and I went into his room to study and I found that he didn't know some basic grammar. I popped off again and criticized his school. It upset Nathan that I was being short with him for his lack of understanding. So I marched out of that room and went to kiss Christopher good night. He still had his light on and hadn't gotten ready for bed. Because I scolded Christopher *he* was soon upset and didn't want me to read him a story *or* pray with him—he wanted Mommy.

Within 20 minutes I'd violated the basic biblical principle—do not provoke your children to anger—three times! So Jennifer took the role of the soother, going to each of the boys, saying, "You know that Daddy hasn't been feeling well and today he is like a short-fused firecracker. He isn't really upset with any of you. He isn't feeling well and when Daddy doesn't eat, his patience has a shorter fuse."

Then she came to me to point out my behavior. Even though I was sick, that did not give me license to accuse the boys unjustly. I had been picking on their splinters, but I hadn't recognized my own log. I went downstairs and asked forgiveness of Joshua for accusing him. Then I went into Nathan's room and asked forgiveness for criticizing his school. Finally, I went to Christopher and he allowed me to read him a story, even though it was later than he was usually allowed to stay up.

Again, when you are truthful with yourself, things can be resolved so easily. It is when you fight and kick and try to defend your position that you find problems. When you try to see things from the other person's position it's so easy and so simple. I wish I would follow my own advice all the time!

Many times I know what I should do in confessing and asking forgiveness, yet I don't do it quickly. And when I *do* ask for forgiveness, I wonder why I waited so long. On an evaluation we had sent to the wives to comment on the FATHERS Ministry, one woman wrote: "I can never remember my parents ever asking for my forgiveness when there was strife and when they had wronged us." I wish that every family knew how easy it can be, rather than holding in the anger and resentment and defensiveness.

Joshua and Nathan and Christopher know that they have a daddy who fails and who needs their forgiveness. Because they have heard me confess my failures, they know that it is all right for them to fail and to confess and forgive each other.

104

One evening two children were sitting together on their living-room couch, while FATHERS member Bill was working on the family checkbook. It seems that the kids weren't enjoying this time together, because Bill continually heard, "David is on my side" and "Abigail's touching me!" Their father was long-suffering for just so long. Finally he administered the "laying on of hands" and sent them to their rooms. A short time later he was going upstairs to conclude the period of discipline with reconciliation and a hug when he heard David saying, "I'm sorry, Abigail, will you forgive me?" And the equally tearful Abigail replied, "Oh, yes, David, and I'm sorry too. Will you forgive me?" They had learned the joy of forgiveness and reconciliation for themselves.

In another context, at each FATHERS meeting, a latecomer will simply ask for forgiveness and the whole group will say, "You are forgiven." Then we will proceed with the meeting. I wish every person in the world could learn to admit error and admit it so quickly and easily—and then to experience a whole group's forgiveness. There is power in forgiveness and it needs to be just as easy as that.

Letting the Children Lead Us

I think one of the best things we can do is to encourage our children to talk about their day, and listen, really listen. What was fun? What was boring? Who got into trouble at school and how did they feel about it? Who was mean to them and why do they think that person behaved that way? And always, what can we learn about Jesus and His love for us in today's events?

Letting the children lead me is my primary objective at bedtime. Let them say whatever comes into their heads without fear of rejection—this isn't the time for scolding because of the day's misbehavior or a messy room. Let the child express any feelings of hurt or anger that have been held throughout the day and then bring those feelings to Jesus. Remember Ephesians 4:26: "Be angry but do not sin; do not let the sun go down on your anger, and give no opportunity to the devil."

As they were talking at bedtime one evening, Carl's son Ben said he didn't want to go to school the next day; he was tired of school. As they began to explore that desire it came out that he didn't want to go on an upcoming field trip to the zoo either, which was very strange, because Ben loves to go to the zoo. They talked a bit about these feelings and Carl discovered that Ben was worried that he wouldn't be able to walk with his friends or that he would have to sit with somebody he didn't like on the bus. So Carl suggested some creative alternatives: maybe Ben could choose someone new to walk with or get to know a new friend. They also talked about some questions he could ask of whomever he sat with or walked beside. Their conversation led to greater reassurance so they prayed about the zoo trip and Ben went to sleep looking forward to the next day.

Dark Thoughts

At one time or another, almost every child has a fear of the dark or a fear of being alone. That fear can be an opportunity for spiritual growth and worship together.

During the weeks following Halloween, one family was troubled by their six-year-old who was afraid to go down the hallway to the bathroom. He wanted not only a nightlight in his room, but insisted that the light be left on in the hallway, which disturbed his older sister.

What were they to do? First they encouraged their son

by saying, "Peter, we're sitting right out here. Go to the bathroom!" Then they tried, "So you're scared of imaginary monsters? You see this spanker? We'll give you something to be scared about!" That approach certainly didn't work so they tried to draw on lessons that Peter had already learned.

"Peter," Mom asked, "where is this fear of yours? Is it behind the shower curtain or under the sink?"

"No," said Peter, "I know it's in my imagination."

"And who is with you while Mom and Dad are in another room?"

"Mom," explained Peter, "my head knows that Jesus is with me, but my tummy is still scared."

So Mom decided to use his sanctified imagination. "Peter, your imagination is making monsters, so use your imagination to make funny monsters instead of scary ones. Can you imagine a pink monster with a big ugly nose? Now imagine that big pink monster crying and running away from your pet hamster!"

Peter was giggling in no time and there were no more problems with the monsters in the bathroom. Later that evening, Mom and Dad and Sister and Peter all thanked Jesus for teaching them how not to be scared of imaginary monsters.

Not long ago a sick raccoon wandered up from the woods and sat on our screened porch. This wounded woods creature evoked much sympathy and concern from the boys as they considered how we could best help him recover. Jennifer was alone that day with the boys, who became very excited about nursing the raccoon. There was also our dog who barked and jumped at the door. He had his own sort of ideas about what he would like to do with the raccoon! This all happened on a day that Jennifer had set aside to have a quiet time of preparation for a Bible study she was to lead the next week.

For nine hours Jennifer's day was completely occupied with this raccoon. There were phone calls to the zoo, to zoo volunteers, to the SPCA and to friends who she thought might be able to help. Late in the afternoon I dashed in, offered some very helpful advice (which Jennifer did not seem to appreciate) and dashed out again to another appointment.

Finally, by eight o'clock that night, the raccoon had limped off and Jennifer thought she could get the boys to bed and have some time for study. As she was just sitting down with her Bible and notes, she heard Chris calling down the stairs. "Mom," whined the little voice, "what if the raccoon climbs on the roof and gets in my window? I'm scared!"

Remembering a precept of child psychology, Jennifer yelled from the living room, "Christopher, you are in charge of your own mind! Tell your mind that there is nothing to be afraid of and *go to sleep!*"

When she sat down and opened her study guide, this is exactly what she read: "One of the times when we can demonstrate our part in child raising is when our children are frightened. When fear crouches at the foot of my child's bed, I use the situation to point him to God."[3]

As Jennifer says, that was one great opportunity that slipped right by.

Spiritual Times, Ordinary Times

What do you think were the most spiritual moments in Jesus' life? Jennifer and I tried to list just a few to see which ones might be labeled the most spiritual.

Certainly we thought that a very spiritual time in Jesus'

early life would have been that day when, as a 12-year-old, He sat with the elders in the Temple. As an adult, undoubtedly a very spiritual time for Jesus was when He spent an entire night alone in prayer, seeking the Father's guidance in choosing 12 among His followers to be the special disciples. (I've led several series for our FATHERS members on prayer and I know how difficult prayer can be, as well as how rewarding.) What about John 3, when Jesus told Nicodemus that one had to be born again to enter the Kingdom? Or recall John 4 where Jesus talked with the woman at the well in Samaria. These would rate at the top of the list.

"What about that morning after the Resurrection," Jennifer suggested, "when the Lord cooked fish and prepared breakfast for the disciples?"

"Cooking breakfast? What's spiritual about cooking breakfast?" I asked.

"Well," she said, "it seems to me that Jesus used that opportunity to minister to the needs the men had right then—food and a warm fire. That was an expression of caring, providing and of His presence with them. That seems very spiritual to me."

"If we include something like that," I said thoughtfully, "then we'd also have to consider the time He washed the disciples' feet."

"And when He let the woman wash His own feet as well as when Mary persuaded Him to make wine in Cana," added Jennifer.

"I don't know, Jennifer. Jesus had sort of a disagreement with Mary about the wine at Cana. It almost looks as though we're saying that a family argument can be a spiritual time."

"Well, why not?" Jennifer questioned.

The more Jennifer and I studied and talked, the harder

it seemed to be able to separate the spiritual times of Jesus' life from the "ordinary" times. Everything He did, from eating and washing to praying and healing in the Temple, was a spiritual action in one way or another. Then we thought about our own lives. Were we mistaken in thinking of the spiritual times as separate from the ordinary things we do every day?

What are our most spiritual moments? Is it when we are having family devotions or is it when we've had a disagreement, maybe even yelled at each other, and we come back to say, "I'm sorry. Will you forgive me?"

FATHERS member Michael usually takes his family out each week to see a movie or sports event. When they come home, they make a fire in the fireplace and pop popcorn. During one of these evenings, little Billy made a real pest of himself in the car on the drive home, so he was punished by being sent to sit in his bedroom while the rest of the family had popcorn. After the family had the fire going and the popcorn ready, Michael went back to Billy's room and said, "You go on out with the others. I'll stay here and take your punishment." Through Michael's action the entire family experienced a vivid example of what Jesus did for everyone.

Was our best spiritual experience last Christmas when we sat together in the midnight caroling service? Or was it when we were driving together to the shopping mall and got stuck in a traffic jam on the interstate? Maybe it was the time we had guests in for Sunday evening supper and had cheese sandwiches and tomato soup. If we fail to realize that every moment of every day is an opportunity to recognize the Spirit's work in our lives, we are missing our goal of living by the Spirit.

Some time ago Joshua was invited to a church party at a favorite pizza restaurant. I drove Joshua to the church parking lot, where the kids were getting into vans, and I carefully made arrangements to see that he would have a ride back home. I also gave him two quarters to keep in case he had to make a telephone call.

Lo and behold, along about 11:00 I got a telephone call and it was Joshua, saying, "I've been left here." The youth leader thought that Joshua had gone home with someone else. So I drove out to pick him up. On the way back home we talked and found the situation very enlightening. "Well, how did you feel when you realized that you were left without a ride home?" I asked.

"I was a little scared," he admitted, "and then I remembered that you had given me the money to make a call. But I wondered if you'd mind coming this late to pick me up."

I said, "But that's what fathers are to do, to protect their children and to watch over them. That's why I gave you the money in the first place and why I'm glad to come." Our prayers that night were very special, thanking God for providing for us ahead of time and for meeting us in our particular need.

Later, it occurred to me how easy it might have been for Joshua to remember those quarters and to think, "Aw, I won't need these,"—and to be tempted to use them to buy extra game tokens. I think about how God has given us gifts that He knows we will need sometime in life and in ways we may not be able to imagine now.

These are examples of how we recognize spiritual realities in our ordinary experiences. Jesus is not a dualist, separating holy things from ordinary things, the spiritual from the physical. He does not isolate religion into certain sanctified times or places. He know that all of life is one piece, one whole. Life in the Spirit should take place in every home and in every moment of every day.

The Family Spiritual Quilt

Jennifer suggests that our family's spirituality can be represented by an old quilt that my grandmother made for us. Grandma Josie was 98 when she died and her quilt is more precious to us than anyone can imagine from looking at it. Like all things of the Spirit, its worth isn't visible to the human eye and it can't be judged in terms of financial value.

Grandma Josie's quilt is made up of ordinary patches of corduroy, knit together with cotton yarn. When common experiences are knit together by the thread of commitment to live out Jesus' life and love in our total everyday experiences, we are making a family spiritual quilt that will stay with us forever.

There are a few patches on Grandma's quilt that are decorated by an embroidered flower or a special ornament. These seem to represent the special times and are in the minority, maybe one out of a dozen plain patches. In reality, family spirituality consists of the ordinary bits and pieces of time that we miss if we only look at the special times.

When sitting around the table together or maybe in the car during a trip, discuss those times that stand out in your minds when you have seen God at work in your family. As you gather these remembrances, you will be forming your own family spiritual quilt. And as you do this, thank God for the working of His Spirit among all of you in the ordinary *and* special times of your life.

This chapter began with a story about a woman who lost something valuable without realizing her loss. It seems appropriate to end with a similar story that has a different ending.

Jennifer was shopping in the meat section of the market when she realized that the diamond from her engagement ring was missing. She exclaimed in surprise, and when the butcher heard what the matter was, he sympathized. He had lost the stone from his ring one time, he said, while making up a batch of ham salad. Two days later a customer had found it in a sandwich and returned it to him!

Well, Jennifer didn't want to go searching through piles of ham salad or crawl around in the aisles of the supermarket. In fact, the stone would be difficult to find because we had been engaged during my seminary years and the diamond I was able to give her was not exactly "the rock of ages."

When she told me what had happened we sat down with Josh, who was three at the time, to pray. "Lord, we thank you that our lives aren't bound up in material things. But you know that my diamond is an expression of love. So we ask for your wisdom and providence in helping us find this diamond."

Later that day Jennifer called us into the kitchen. "I was cleaning up around the house and I found my Bible lying on the table where I'd left it this morning. I picked up the Bible and look what was right beneath it!" It was her diamond.

If you had asked my three-year-old theologian just then whether God cared about our daily cares and concerns, Josh would answer with an immediate yes! He knew then, and he still knows, that God is present, available and concerned in the everyday joys and problems of our family life.

> Or what woman, having ten silver coins, if
> she loses one coin, does not light a lamp and
> sweep the house and seek diligently until she

finds it? And when she has found it, she calls together her friends and neighbors, saying, "Rejoice with me, for I have found the coin which I had lost." Just so, I tell you, there is joy before the angels of God over one sinner who repents (Luke 15:8-10).

Tips

Scripture memorization is an important part of many families' worship experience. I suggest two methods:

Traditional Scripture Bees. Learn verses by rote, then test one another. See who can recite the most verses correctly, as in a spelling bee.

The Musical Method. Many Psalms, promises and special verses have been set to music. We can hide the Word in our hearts while praising the Lord in song.

Worship in the Children's Bedrooms. Schedule family times of worship in each child's room. Encourage the child whose room you will use to make the necessary preparations and be the leader if he or she desires. Encourage creativity. Be prepared for a rewarding experience and insight into your children's spiritual understanding.

Think Symbolically. Be creative and let your family's imagination run wild as you think of the various church holidays and special seasons you celebrate. Add to your meal table, front door, windows and children's rooms those various symbols and pictures that help to impress upon your family the season's particular religious theme. For instance, on Pentecost the whole family can sometime wear red to church and Sunday School to symbolize the fire of the Holy Spirit. Use nails, a hammer, a crown of thorns, vinegar, a sponge, etc., for decorating during Lent.

TAKING INVENTORY

1. What do you believe are some prerequisites to (a) personal worship, (b) family worship?

2. Complete the following statement with at least five answers: Family worship is . . . .

3. What are your thoughts concerning a father's role in the family's spiritual development? In what ways do you take the initiative for your family's spiritual development?

4. What specific things could you do to nurture your family's worship times?

5. How many creative ways can you list to worship the Lord as a family? What can each family member do to contribute to a time of worship? What are some of the family's favorite hymns, choruses, songs, Bible stories, passages?

6. What have you found to be the single most important facilitator to conducting regular family worship? What are the main barriers? Discuss ways to overcome these barriers.

7. When do you believe is the best time for your family to have a time of worship? When do you get together as a family to sing hymns, to pray together, to praise the Lord or to read Scriptures? When did you last get together and do any of the above?

8. Share a meaningful worship experience you and your family have had recently. What specific family prayers have been answered? Comment on these.

Chapter 7

Giving Thanks and Encouragement

Then one of them, when he saw that he was healed, turned back, praising God with a loud voice; and he fell on his face at Jesus' feet, giving him thanks (Luke 17:15-16).

What do you have to be thankful for? Have you expressed your thanksgiving in such a way that the people you love are aware of your feelings? There are times when I look at my kids playing ball or just sitting around in the family room and I am so overwhelmed with gratitude that I don't know what to do. God has indeed been good to Jennifer and me. But I admit that I have difficulty expressing not only my gratitude to God, but my appreciation of those persons I love.

Consider the story found in Luke 7:36. A woman came into the home of Simon, the Pharisee, from the streets. She washed Jesus' feet, kissed them and dried them with her hair. Simon was critical, but Jesus said to him, "Do you see this woman?"

The story continues and the woman is forgiven while Simon is chastized. Please notice Jesus' pertinent question: "Do you see this woman?" The Pharisee saw her in light of her role in society—as a prostitute. Jesus saw an individual with specific value and special needs.

Recall how the Lord noticed Zacchaeus up in a tree? (See Luke 19:1-10.) Life was changed because Jesus saw what Zacchaeus could become and affirmed him, while others only condemned him.

There is also the story of the widow woman in the Temple who gave two pennies to the treasury. (See Luke 21:1-4). Jesus noticed and affirmed her in her action.

Jesus saw people as they truly were, just as He sees us and values us for what we truly are.

Do we see our kids as individuals? Or do we see them only as "the kids"? Do we really know who they are as unique persons or only in the role they play in our own lives? Jennifer and I want to be absolutely certain that each son knows, as he grows, that he is a special and wonderful person with precious gifts from God. There is only one of his kind. One of the things we do during times of family worship around the dinner table to foster this understanding is to thank God for each member and affirm each person for his or her own uniqueness.

I have had the opportunity to present chapel services for some of the professional baseball teams that come to Riverfront Stadium to play the Reds. Through these services I've developed a friendship with Doug Rau, who was a pitcher for the Los Angeles Dodgers. One afternoon we invited him and his wife Rhonda to our home for a late lunch. I waited outside the stadium with my boys, who bounced with excitement.

When Doug and Rhonda came out to the car, the boys were shocked. Who was this stranger in a blue turtleneck and jeans? They didn't recognize their hero without his uniform. They knew him so well from a distance, but they didn't know *him* at all.

Earlier that same day Jennifer had been feeling some anxiety, wondering, "What do I serve to these celebrities? What do I say to a wife of a professional ball player? How will I talk with her?"

After we sat down and got to know each other as persons, Rhonda confessed that she had been anxious about meeting Jennifer, wondering, "What in the world will I say to this preacher's wife!"

We'd been afraid of the image each of us portrayed, forgetting the unique individual.

Ordinary and Special

We need to affirm each other in the ordinary situations and during the special occasions. On the day that the report cards come home, I might say to Christopher, "Son, I see that you have two *A*s and a *B* on your report card and I want to affirm the good work that you've done these past six weeks. I feel very proud of your grades and your choice to really use the gifts of intelligence and perseverance that God has given you." That would be an affirmation in a special time.

Another day I might say, "Joshua, I heard you talking with your friend and you were angry with him. I heard you expressing your feelings and talking with him in such a way that in a few minutes the anger was gone and you were in a good relationship again. I just want to affirm you in that and recognize your effort to live out the principles you've been taught about good relationships."

My affirmation might be very simple, as when I say to Jennifer, "Honey, I know you had to wait at the license bureau and experience the frustration of getting new tags for the car. On top of that, you went grocery shopping alone and put a lot of effort toward making dinner. I really appreciate it. I affirm your gifts of patience and faithfulness to us."

Do you remember to express your appreciation to your wife and kids? Do they know that you love them and that you notice the little things they do? Or do you let them assume too much?

Encouragement

I coached T-Ball for nine years, giving three years to each son (who conveniently have birthdays three years apart). We taught those five-to-eight year olds the fundamentals of baseball and also some of the fundamentals of life. But in my coaching career, the *most* important lesson was that of encouragement.

At the start of every season I always met with the parents, explaining that my purpose in coaching was to encourage these boys and girls and to provide a good experience with a sport. I did not yell at them and did not permit parents to yell at any child except in encouragement. I told the parents that I would personally go over to the rooters' section and sit with them, reminding them of this principle if they slipped. I trained my other coaches to always get down on their knees during practice so they could look the child in the eyes, and with a smile on their face affirm what he/she was able to do. We also made an effort to put a hand or arm around their shoulder, tousle their hair and give a quick hug. We believed in that type of affirming contact, for we not only gained the trust of the child but we earned the right to be heard when we needed to give suggestions and corrections.

Sometimes it was so hard to find something encouraging to say to these children that it bordered on the ridiculous. I remember one game in particular. The dad coaching first base was frustrated with one of our players, yet so determined to be affirming that he hollered, "Way to kick the dirt, son, that's the way to get the dirt out of the way!"

We also celebrated the "Stars of the Game." Each parent would take turns bringing pop to celebrate the game and we would place the cooler out in front of the bench where the players sat. As the families gathered around their own son or daughter, the coaches and myself would kneel around the cooler and call each player up to receive pop due to some particular play or good thing the child had done during that game. Each of those kids would hop off that bench, receive their pop (with everyone cheering and clapping) and hop back on the bench, as proud as if they'd won the World Series trophy!

When it came down to championship times, we asked a Boy Scout troop to display the flag and a soprano to sing the "Star Spangled Banner." We always brought a bullhorn and announced each child's name as he/she ran onto the field, making each player feel important before and after each game.

I think one of my greatest contributions was working with the director of the local leagues, convincing him and the board that we should present trophies to every child who participated in T-Ball. It was a joy to go to play-off and championship games and see the coaches giving a trophy and a handshake to every child—including those on the losing teams. Even if a team had a 0-12 record, the losses were quickly absorbed in the joy of receiving a trophy.

Because we affirmed our boys and girls, they sensed the difference as parents and coaches on other teams would yell derogatories or get very upset with their kids if they struck out or didn't do something. Many parents have commented that as their child began playing football or soccer in high school, they would invariably make a comparison to their T-Ball experience and say, "Coach Rand would not have done this. And our coaches would not have yelled like that." Our prayer time together and simple Bible study with each of our sons made a difference.

After coaching for nine years, I was privileged to coach a championship team with my children in the final year. And I know that was no accident. I firmly believe that under the fruit of encouragement, our teams always peaked at the end of the season because the boys and girls believed in themselves. You can't convince me that it was my coaching prowess, because all of our kids weren't outstanding players. They knew that we believed in them, win or lose, so they could not fail.

The Fruits of Encouragement

Christians are called to encourage one another. Encouragement in Greek is *paracletis,* also translated as comfort. The name given to the Holy Spirit in the Gospel of John is the Paraclete, the Comforter or Encourager. Encouragement is intimately related to the ministry of the Holy Spirit, so when we minister encouragement to one another we are ministering the power of the Holy Spirit. Encouragement takes different forms: in our words, through our hands, by our presence and in our writing.

Encouragement in Our Words. A long time ago we began a tradition of passing a candle after supper in our home on Thursday nights. We light a candle at the end of the meal and pass it to a child. As the candle is passed, we call that child by name and affirm something special about him. Then every other member of the family affirms that child and is, in turn, themselves affirmed.

Many times our boys have come to the table squabbling and calling each other names (heaven forbid, in a pastor's home!). During the meal some residue of feeling usually remains. But when we pass the candle, feelings are confessed and forgiven and it is a beautiful thing to hear the children affirming one another.

Naturally, family affirmation was awkward at first and became more natural and meaningful only as the practice developed into a tradition. Early on, each of the boys would affirm Mom's good cooking (although they hadn't eaten anything) and maybe Dad's hard work. They gradually learned to be more personal. Now Christopher, the youngest, might pass the candle to Joshua saying, "I affirm the time you play with me and make me feel important." Nathan might say to Christopher, "I affirm your creativity in the great project you made for school."

Many times pastors do not affirm lay people and vice versa. Too often we come home on Sunday and have roast pastor for dinner. In response we have adopted the passing of the candle in our various activities at church. Small groups are often seen passing a candle to one another and affirming each member. This ministers deeply to both lay persons and clergy who attend our many evangelism and equipping classes—and also to our denominational executives who frequently visit our programs. Our teams look for every opportunity to encourage and affirm every person.

We aren't often aware that persons in "positions of power and prestige" can be terribly lonely and isolated from support groups available in the local parish. A denominational leader in evangelism from the Presbyterian Church, USA, came to our evangelism seminars saying he would prefer to stay in a hotel instead of a home so he could be alone to write. One of our families was going to be away during the clinic and suggested that he might stay there. Their home was within walking distance of the church and had a study and quiet garden—the perfect atmosphere for writing. At one point in the seminars he joined my small group and we passed a candle to him. As we were all affirming him, he began to weep. Quietly, he confessed that he felt like the loneliest person in New York City. Even though he worked at the great multidenominational church center, it seemed that church work had sometimes taken precedence over one of the important aspects of the work of the Church, that is, personal affirmation and fellowship. The encouragement he felt in the seminar had touched his heart.

Another family on the team took this leader into their home for the remaining days of the program so he could have full-time fellowship. In the years since that time, he and his family have returned periodically to Cincinnati and have developed deep and lasting ties with our congregation.

Encouragement Through Our Hands. Sometimes encouragement can be just a pat on the shoulder as you walk past. Other times you can give a back rub, a shoulder massage or some other nonpossessive touch that lets someone understand what you might find difficult to say. You can also allow others to touch you by using words such as, "Here, would you help me with this tie?" or "Would you rub my shoulder? It feels so stiff." Encouraging by means of touch is particularly good in communicating to teenagers your love for them. All of these suggestions are little ways of touching that encourage others in a big way.

Encouragement by Our Presence. Presence is the comfort you give when there is nothing to be done or said. It may involve staying up late with a child while she finishes her homework, being a companion in the hospital waiting room or preparing a cup of tea after bad news arrives. Ministers learn how important presence can be, but lay people can minister just as effectively. There is no requirement other than a willingness to *be there*.

Encouragement in Our Writing. When there are deep or troubled feelings, sometimes a card or a letter may communicate better than the spoken word. College students, military personnel, missionaries and family members who live far apart can all be blessed by a personal note of encouragement. Or when presence is impossible and the spoken word is awkward, the written word can touch someone who hurts. During times of grief, when visitations are over and relatives have left the home, the mourning family may pick up the cards and notes and receive a comfort that can be tucked away and read over and over in the lonely times.

A friend who lost a spouse after a long and tragic illness was asked to speak to seminarians about how to minister to the bereaved. "What do you say," they wanted to know, "when there are really no words to say?" The bereaved person gave two examples of notes that gave the needed comfort:

> I just heard of Sandy's death. We share a love few friends ever know and I want you to know that I am hurting with you.
>
> I've thought of you a lot since your loved one died. Knowing you, I imagine you have a lot of thoughts and feelings going around and around, now that the sickness is over and Sandy is gone. I wish I was there to listen and share my own thoughts with you. I hope someone is.

There is no attempt in these notes to explain or excuse

the death, no pretense at turning sorrow into happiness. Here are simple words of encouragement—words that let a person know someone cares.

We All Need Encouragement

Who needs encouragement? Parents need to be encouraged in the everyday chores of life. Little children who think, "I can't do anything right," need to be encouraged. Young people who feel alone and rejected by the crowd need encouragement. Individuals facing illness, the possibility of their own death or the terminal illness of someone they love need encouragement. Ministers and Christian workers need encouragement. It is more difficult to think of someone who does *not* need encouragement.

Encouragement Combats Depression

Not long ago I was surprised to learn that Charles Spurgeon, the great teacher and evangelist, was haunted by discouragement. He often gave two sermons each Sunday to crowded churches, only to return home late at night and fall into what might be diagnosed today as a manic-depressive state. He would hear the voice of Satan laughing at him: "Ha, you preached all those sermons and what difference does it make? What difference?"

Charles Spurgeon, a giant of the faith, discouraged? Who else then, among our Christian leaders, might be subject to despair? Pastors and teachers and lay leaders and youth workers *all* need brothers and sisters who will take time to offer a word, a touch or a note of encouragement and thanks.

Depression is more common than most of us realize. We often hear of women who are depressed, but men are also afflicted—although perhaps they are less willing to admit it. Severe depression needs professional attention and I urge spouses and families to provide that help since the victims of depression may not be able to seek out help themselves.

Brian is an elder in our congregation and a scientist by profession with a major corporation. At one time he suffered severe depression and was hospitalized. During the months of his recovery, our prayer and support group upheld him and his family many times. In fact, we literally "upheld" him once. On that particular evening Brian said that he felt so miserable he could lay down on the basement floor and that still wouldn't be low enough. So he did; he lay face down on the floor. We then gathered around Brian and as we prayed, we gently lifted him up, higher and higher until he almost touched the joists of the basement ceiling. It was a concrete expression of our spiritual support. Today, after much help, Brian is well and whole, a strong member of the community and congregation.

The ministry of encouragement can bless, heal, encourage and break down barriers. I see it working daily in the home, at T-Ball, in the church and in the heirarchy of the Church. Encouragement is without any doubt the work of the Holy Spirit, the Comforter. May each of us learn to be His hands, His mouth and His presence to the ones we love.

The Ideal American Couple

Bruce and Janet grew up together in a small town where everybody knew everybody. They went to the same high school and confessed their faith in the same eighth grade communicants' class. They were married shortly before Bruce went off to Korea as a fighter pilot. To any casual observer, they appeared to be the ideal American couple.

After Bruce came home, twin boys were born. But one of the babies had multiple birth defects. Bruce and Janet became bitterly angry with God. What had happened to their ideal life? How could He have done this to their baby?

Two more boys were born as the years went by and Bruce and Janet seemed to be doing fine. They didn't turn to alcohol or drugs. They even went back to church because they knew that the children, especially their handicapped boy, would need God. But too many dreams weren't coming true, too many hurts were tucked away and never faced.

Then in 1974, things fell apart. The boys, now teenagers, became involved in the local drug scene. Pressures in Bruce's job increased and one thing led to another. The ideal American couple got an American divorce just before their twenty-fifth anniversary.

Bruce says in retrospect that although they considered themselves Christians, it was obvious that they knew nothing about Jesus as Lord. Their ideal American home was built on sand. In his words, they were "conventional and dull enough to get along for awhile, but when the going got tough, it all collapsed." But the Lord is patient and merciful and forgiving. He first drew Janet and then Bruce slowly to Himself. Then He showed them a new congregation, where they heard—and *really* understood—what it means to be obedient to God. In 1982, nine years after their divorce, they were remarried. As they now testify together, they realize how very much they have for which to be thankful.

Dealing with Crisis

Always and for everything giving thanks in the

name of our Lord Jesus Christ to God the
Father (Eph. 5:20).

These verses present a theological problem for some
people, as does the statement in Romans 8:28 that says
that God works in everything for good. Once, after I had
preached on this verse, I was challenged by some people
who said that it is one thing to give thanks *in* everything,
but quite different to give thanks *for* everything. It is
wrong, they said, to thank God *for* evil. We should be
thankful *in* evil circumstances. When they pointed out 1
Thessalonians 5:18, which speaks about giving thanks *in*
all circumstances, I was able to show that Ephesians 5:20
used the prepositions *for.*

The real question is not which preposition to use—*in*
or *for*—but rather, why does God allow suffering? It is my
understanding that suffering is a part of our environment in
this world. God has put us here at risk of injury as we
learn the things of life from trial and error. Our belief
should reflect the understanding that whatever natural
consequences of sin or tragedy might occur, God will bring
blessings in spite of it all. We base our belief that God
"works to good" on knowing God's character—that is,
Who He is. Because God is Who He is, we can trust Him
in, for, through, with (insert any possible preposition) all
circumstances.

It is possible for God to take a crisis or a difficulty and
bring about a greater good. I do not believe that God
causes evil to afflict us, but He will sometimes allow evil to
occur. God did not afflict Job—Satan did that. God brought
greater blessing to Job in his latter days. There are physical forces and natural consequences of actions from which
God does not always protect us. But He will bless us in
spite of all this, if we give Him the opportunity by our

faith. Could it be that we have failed in gratitude by refusing to see blessing in the darkness of tragedy?

Two men come to my mind as vivid examples of God's work in crisis and tragedy. David Tedford has been a member of the FATHERS Ministry since 1981. In August 1983, a waterskiing accident virtually severed David's left hand at the wrist. Connected only by a small piece of flesh, and against the advice of doctors who doubted the hand could be reattached, David begged for surgery to try to save his hand. Three surgeries followed in close succession to reconstruct the bones, tendons, nerves and tissues. Slow, painful and discouraging therapy lasted for a year and a half.

David explains that the FATHERS Ministry and the prayer support of the whole Christian community "became my left hand during this time. I am totally convinced that the prayers of God's people made the difference for me."

David's hand now appears completely normal with movement restored in all his fingers. David testifies that God is continually present in and through crisis to uphold, heal and restore.

John Benson's testimony is quite different. Severely burned over 50 percent of his body in an automobile accident, John lost one leg and all of the fingers on one hand. He also has a severely scarred face. Like David Tedford, John was a committed Christian before the accident, but his life hadn't been "the bowl of cherries" we seem to expect from the Christian faith. For three years, John had faced setbacks in his job, problems in his marriage and a lack of direction for his life. The auto accident was the culmination of a confusing series of frustrations.

As he lay in the hospital close to death, with bandages covering his face and most of his body, John realized that he was praying out loud. Without understanding why, he found himself surrendering his life, his future and what was left of his body to the Lord, to do whatever God chose to do with him—even to the point of facing the fire again. At that point, John believes a great healing of his spirit began.

It was through his "trial by fire" that John found purpose to his life. The surrounding community of believers embraced and expressed the concern and care of the Father so completely that John is healed in the furthest depths of his soul. John explains that he is more complete as a man today than before the accident, because God is working in and through his life. His profession now involves providing prosthetic limbs to other amputees and witnessing to the power of Jesus Christ, who makes crippled spirits whole.

Giving thanks to God in the ordinary times, in the special times and in the difficult times—this is what it means to live a life of thankfulness to God. I believe that we need to learn to look at all these times together and say to our children, "See, this was when God touched us and that was the time when we were blessed."

Poodles and Basset Hounds

Along with being thankful and encouraging to one another, let's give permission to each other to be ourselves, for we are as unique in personality and temperament as we are in physical appearance. I realize that grouchiness is not a particularly desirable quality and depression is not always a healthy state of mind, but it's also good to remember that perpetual cheerfulness is not necessarily God's standard for all Christians.

You know how sad basset hounds seem and how perky poodles appear? How dull the world would be if all the basset hounds became poodles! And how dull it would be if all Christian mothers, fathers and children thought they had to be cheerful all the time! Yet we sometimes think that Christians must always be cheerful and lighthearted, never feeling the heaviness of life's reality. If we truly affirm that all reality is God's good creation, then we can permit ourselves and others to experience the feelings of that creation in all tones and shading—and to be thankful that He created us this way.

What do we have for which to be thankful? We have our families, friends, health, feelings, jobs, homes, our country and ourselves, just the way we are. Are we willing to look at all that we have and be like the man who, when he saw that he was healed, turned back, praised God with a loud voice and fell on his face at Jesus' feet, giving Him thanks?

Tips

The child that pulls away from a hug is probably the child that needs it the most. You don't want to force it in any way, but you can help that child receive affection by other, less-threatening contacts: a pat on the shoulder, a quick squeeze on the knee when sitting together, a ruffling of the hair or a shoulder or back massage. Ask the child to teach you the latest "hand jive," challenge her to arm wrestle or dare him to try to pick up the "old man!" Say that you bet she can't knock you off balance using only her hands against your hands—then let her do it. The more physical contact the child has, the easier it will be to accept physical expressions of affection.

Each Child Should Have a Day. The special day should be announced and adhered to. This will build self-confidence and leadership.

Good Thing of the Day. Encourage each family member to share one good thing of the day at mealtime. Each family member must be instructed to listen attentively and not interrupt. Allow for the reality that some days are filled with things that are not good. Also encourage everyone to share their hurts, concerns and pains.

TAKING INVENTORY

1. List five character or personality traits about which you can affirm each of your children. Tell each family member one special trait you see in them each day and why you are thankful for them.

2. Consider some of the mistakes you have made in your lifetime and from which you have learned some lessons. Consider revealing these to your children. This process will help make you more approachable and affirm your children when they make mistakes.

3. What are some of the things that differentiate a house from a home? What are some of the specific things that make your house a home? Discuss this topic with your family and use it as a means of affirming each family member for his/her part in making your home.

4. List your own talent or spiritual gifts and those of each family member. Ask each family member to make the same two lists. Share those lists and compare.

5. Do you have a family ritual such as a flower, meal or plate to recognize special occasions or achievements? Establish some traditions for successful praise, thanksgiving and affirmation activities in your home.

6. Have you ever memorized or taught your children a verse of Scripture which speaks to thanksgiving? If so, which verses have been meaningful?
   Example 1: In everything give thanks: for this is the will of God in Christ Jesus concerning you. (See 1 Thess. 5:18.)
   Example 2: But Godliness with contentment is great gain. (See 1 Tim. 6:6.)

7. Do my children see an attitude of thanksgiving in my life?

Chapter 8

Creating Family Fun Times

The point is this: he who sows sparingly will also reap sparingly, and he who sows bountifully will also reap bountifully (2 Cor. 9:6).

There is a threefold purpose to this chapter. First, to demonstrate how to provide experiences for your children so they will have fond memories of the family doing and experiencing things together. When they are older, we hope they will not look back on a void, recalling only their own individual conquests.

Second, this chapter will emphasize the importance of establishing roots to help each family member have a secure identity. We hope that each child will build his/her identity not only as a unique individual, but also as a member of a family with a meaningful heritage and all that is implied in the expression, "having roots."

Third, I hope to reflect upon family traditions, again with the goal of providing good memories. It seems that much of the ministry of counseling and healing of memories concerns the repairing of past family failures. Our family night theme may be thought of as preventative medicine: building memories *now* that will minimize the need for healing *later.*

Edith Schaeffer comments, "What is a family meant to be? Among other things, I personally have always felt it is meant to be a museum of memories—collections of carefully preserved memories. Someone in the family . . . needs to be conscious that memories are important. Memories (not all of them, but some of them) should be planned with the same careful kind of planning one would give to designing a museum."[1]

Make the Most of This Time

There is a tendency to think nostalgically of the past or wishfully of the future, forgetting that today is God's new gift: "*This* is the day which the LORD has made; let us *rejoice* and be glad in it" (Ps. 118:24, italics added). Let go of the "if onlys" and the "someday whens" and make the most of the present—not as we wish it could have been or what we hope it might be someday. Focus on your family today—whether you are a single parent, a stepmom or dad, a member of a small family of two or three or part of an extended family with grandparents, aunts and uncles and multiple "adopted" members.

While I recognize that it's important for parents to have individual interests and friends, in this chapter I want to emphasize doing things together. In areas where we are accustomed to think of individual involvements, FATHERS members are learning to think in terms of family: family athletics like bowling or golfing, family social groups and even family business trips.

Vacations

Vacations are always special family times. When I was a boy, every summer we went to the national park and hiked. We would get tired together and enjoy God's beauty together. My sister worked in Glacier National Park and she was able to take us to spots where visitors normally do not go. Our mother has asthma, so she would huff and puff her way along and the rest of us learned to set a slower pace to be considerate of her. Some of the Boy Scout badges I received involving forestry and special projects were done as a family on these trips.

I remember those vacations vividly when Jennifer and I plan our vacations now. Jennifer and I have frequently gone to a beach home in Florida. For years the boys liked to play in the sand, build castles, race the surf and chase sea gulls and crabs. But as they have gotten older their interests have changed and they no longer want to visit the beach. Now they want to be at the pool, play video games or find golf balls and snakes on the borders of the golf course. Joshua is talking about possibly taking a friend with him on our next vacation. It's important that we allow family members to be involved in vacation plans. As we try to minister to real needs of family members, our vacation plans change each year.

Sometimes tempers flare on vacations and we try to understand that we might be frazzled from traveling or from being in close quarters for several days. In addition, there is a tendency to look forward in an idealistic way to vacations. Then, when situations are less than ideal, persons can become easily disappointed. So we give one another permission to let off steam in an appropriate manner. Afterwards we ask and give forgiveness so that relationships are quickly mended and the rest of our time is not spoiled by bitterness or guilty feelings.

I find it important to mention that the regular release of emotions is necessary, especially as children approach adolescence and the teen years when stress from peer groups and school becomes intense. In my teen years we played the game Aggravation every night after supper: my dad and I against my mom and Ruth. I would really get aggravated at times and we learned that we could be angry and have healthy fights together over that game. There were times we didn't always say kind words or when someone would slam a fist on the table, knock marbles off the board and stomp out of the room. But we learned to come back when we cooled off, apologize and receive forgiveness. Good family fights over something like a board game can release tensions and frustrations like a steam valve—as well as provide times of fun and pleasure.

Preserving Treasures

Cameras are important in building memories, not only on vacations, birthdays and holidays, but during the week when the family is having good times together. Have you thought of snapping a picture of the baby or toddler taking a nap nestled under the quilt with teddy bears and baby dolls? Or why not catch the kids (when they aren't looking) sitting in the middle of the toys in their rooms or in the sandbox or with peanut butter smeared all over their faces! These sights are commonplace now, but in later years they will restore precious memories.

I suggest getting a tripod and a timer so both parents can be in pictures with the whole family together. When people see the Rand family album they won't ask, "What happened to your father?" or to Jennifer, "Oh, were you a single parent?" With the timer I'm visible now in more pictures. And I'm not shy about asking people to take pictures of us together. Sometimes these willing participants are amateur photographers and maybe they cut my head off a little bit or capture a lot of sky, but at least we have a memory to laugh about together.

When the kids are sick, a father can show special love and care by bringing special presents, books or things that they like. He can also be with them, touch and caress them, take their temperature and simply be there. It's the time to let them sit on your lap, rock in a chair and look through scrapbooks. Sometimes a child is on the move all the time—except when sick. So during those times of earaches, flu or colds, take advantage of those rare opportunities when they may just want to be held quietly. We have also had special times during sickness talking about how they felt about this and did they remember that. These are always special times to build tender and caring memories.

Playing competitive games together enables persons to know one another without our masks. Charades is excellent because it takes no equipment and can be played anywhere with any number or age of participants. Jennifer and I like to portray song titles or movie titles. Of course, as far as the boys are concerned, we're ancient and all the songs and movies we think of are prehistoric! But that leads to good discussions of "When we were kids . . . " and "Remember the time when . . . ?" Or we might pick themes for holidays and seasons of the year, again evoking memories of family experiences, recent and past.

FATHERS members are encouraged to invent new games, share ideas with one another or even join each other's families in playing games together. Sometimes we have gaming tournaments that run for days or weeks, picking up the game each afternoon when the kids get home from school.

Families need to take time to choose memories. As Edith Schaeffer exhorts, "People are involved in the memories, and the togetherness only lasts a certain length of time."[2]

Memorial Stones

And Joshua said to them, "Pass on before the ark of the LORD your God into the midst of the Jordan, and take up each of you a stone upon his shoulder, according to the number of tribes of the people of Israel, that this may be a sign among you, when your children ask in time to come, 'What do those stones mean to you?' Then you shall tell them that the waters of the Jordan were cut off before the ark of the covenant of the LORD . . . . So these stones shall be to the people of Israel a memorial forever (Josh. 4:5-7).

Come to him, to that living stone, rejected by men but in God's sight chosen and precious; and like living stones be yourselves built into a spiritual house, to be a holy priesthood, to offer spiritual sacrifices acceptable to God through Jesus Christ (1 Pet. 2:4-5).

Each year I ask every FATHERS member to select a stone about six inches in diameter during a family outing. On Memorial Day, these stones are used to construct a memorial on the church ground for each class or "generation" of FATHERS. Then we bring our children here on Memorial Day, birthdays, anniversaries or Father's Day to remember that we are a part of this ministry.

The church was in the midst of a major building program when our first generation of FATHERS decided to build their monument. Some smart aleck suggested that we dig a trench and set a wheelbarrow beneath our pillar of cemented stones. That way, if the church happened to expand in the wrong direction, we could dig up the wheelbarrow and move our monument some place else!

Don't Take My Word for It

I thought it would be helpful to ask several fathers to share their ideas about Friday Family Night, so their different experiences and styles would stimulate additional ideas and discussions for you. The following men are a few of those who responded.

George is one of our original FATHERS members, with children now in their teens. He has worked through successes and failures and is a trustworthy resource for men who are just beginning to face difficulties in their own families.

Jason has a son 11 and a daughter 13. He says he's the type that sticks with a problem until he gets it right. He originally made a two-year commitment and is finishing up his fourth year!

Bert has three tiny ones: four years, three years and eight months. Moreover, Bert's 89-year-old grandmother came to make her home with his family just a couple of months back, so he has some important insights on living in a multigenerational family.

Bruce also has preschool girls aged three and five.

David has two boys, thirteen and eight, and a daughter who is six.

Ron: Who wants to get us rolling?

141

David: FATHERS is important to me because it gives us a place to discuss common problems. Fathers of older kids help fathers of younger ones prepare for what they will experience later. It really helps to be able to talk about major decisions involving job changes or buying a house. It also helps to talk about everyday things like roofs that leak. Then there are changing situations as the children are growing up and starting to date or having problems at school—all of that. Most of us don't have our own parents around to look to for help. (And that brings up the problems of aging parents who may live far away.) I know that we've *all* helped each other a lot.

George: David, you've expressed what a lot of us feel, so I'll move right into the Friday Fun Night theme. Because our girls like musicals, we do a lot of that kind of thing. We plan to go to shows, we get the schedules in advance and try to decide which ones we'll like best. There is a special theater where they show the old classic movies, as well as having a tremendous theater organ where our own church organist performs. We get popcorn and the whole works. Also, one of the girls is a cheerleader, so we take the other two to see the home games and that's a new experience for us. At other times we might take seasonal outings: driving to Indiana to see the fall colors, downtown to the Christmas lights or to one of the parks overlooking the river to watch the riverboats come in.

Jason: I agree that older kids are more likely to say, "I don't want to." I've learned to check with the kids, because what *I* think would be fun for the whole family, the kids might decide is really the pits.

But we all like going through the old home movies and slides. And we bought a VCR for Christmas, so a lot of our family fun time lately has been watching films. Last week we watched *Sound of Music* since Sandie is trying out for a part in that play at school. There is a scene in the gazebo, with the girl and boy kissing. My son said he would rather "fast forward" through that mushy stuff and we teased Sandie that she would probably rather "slow motion" through that part!

David: Bike rides are popular with our kids. Joel, who is 13, likes to go out for ice cream. Eight-year-old Stephen likes to wrestle or box. Christy is six and it's hard to find something to do that she particularly likes.

Bert: Our family times are almost always spent at home playing simple board games on the floor. We've severely limited our outside activities, even church things, in order to be home as much as possible.

Ron: Do you ever feel restless being stuck at home with the toddlers every evening?

Bert: Not us. I think it has a lot to do with your attitude: either you want kids or not. If you want them, you don't resent spending evenings with them. Of course I *would* like more evenings out with my wife. Once or twice a month would be great, especially now with my grandmother staying with us.

Bruce: My children are toddlers, too, like Bert's. I've found that at this time, anyway, our goal is to make individuals feel important. Because our girls are small, we tend to have lots of family time naturally, without many outside activities.

Jason: My kids still want to have clubtime—that's something you just don't stop as they get older. They catch me and ask when we're gonna have club this week.

143

It isn't necessarily so formal, with handshakes and stuff. Matt is more of an extrovert and is enthusiastic about anything I suggest. Sandie is more of an introvert and it's sort of difficult to find something that interests her. The other day we needed to do the dishes because Mom and Matt each had to be somewhere in a hurry after supper. Sandie said, "Hey, we're washing dishes together, Daddy. This could be our clubtime for the week." I said, "No, Honey, washing dishes does not count as clubtime!"

Ron: What about floor play, wrestling and that kind of stuff? Do the older kids still like that?

Jason: Actually the kids want more wrestling now than when they were little. Eleven-year-old Matt really likes wrestling and horsing around. Last night he accidently hit me hard on the nose, so I hid my face and carried on about how badly he'd hurt me and how I'd go to work with a black eye. When I had Matt believing me, I tackled him and pinned him to the rug. He loved it.

I remember when I was a kid we watched *Big-Time Wrestling* on TV. Now, Matt gets up early on Saturdays to see Hulk Hogan and those crazy wrestlers, dressed up in far-out costumes. I try to tell him that it's all staged and choreographed to look wilder than it is, but he doesn't care. He wants to get me down and throw me around like Hulk Hogan.

It's harder on me, of course, now that the kids are bigger. I can't pick up or spin them until they're dizzy. *They'd* love it, but *I* just can't! Pretty soon, I think Matt will be able to lift me—at least I let him *think* he will. It's getting hard on the house, too. One of these days we'll break some furniture if this keeps on.

144

Ron: We've talked several times in the squads about physical activities and wrestling with daughters that are beginning to mature. Will anyone share some thoughts on that?

Jason: Sandie is 14 and she wants to wrestle, so we do. Girls need roughhousing as much as the boys—it gets the tension and stress out of their systems, so there is less fussing and arguing around the house. I can't say, "No, you're a girl, so Daddy won't touch you." That would be wrong and she wouldn't understand. It would hurt her. We hear about incest and our kids hear about it, but that's all the more reason that daughters need healthy, nonpossessive touching. As her dad, if I don't touch her in safe, nonsexual ways, expressing affection, she's more likely to get hugs and affection somewhere else where it *won't* be safe.

George: I agree. Wrestling and all that becomes more important as the kids get older—especially with girls. They see all the touching in the media and they need to know that they have a safe place to get hugs. If a dad tells his girl that he thinks she's beautiful, and if she has her hugging needs filled at home, she's not going to be easily tempted by some slick dude. It's easy and natural for my family because we've been a huggy family since they were babies.

Ron: Maybe it would help fathers who worry to say to their daughter, "Honey, if anything I do makes you feel uncomfortable, you let me know." And wrestle in the part of the house where the rest of the family is close by.

George: I also want to say that with teens, their problems can have big consequences and our parental con-

145

cerns are more serious now than when they were small. When disagreements come up, you have to deal more diplomatically. Sometimes we have no choice but to let the kid fail and be hurt. Maybe it's the only way he/she can learn. That's as hard on the parents as on the kid, but it also means that we'll be there later, ready to forgive and help to heal the wounds.

Ron: Bruce, you need to jump in here with your ideas. Take us back to younger children.

Bruce: Well, before FATHERS, I used to exercise my management skills with a list of all the chores that needed to be done. Then on Friday evening or Saturday morning I would go out and follow my efficient plan, trying to get everything done as quickly as possible, while my wife stayed home with the two girls. Now on Saturday mornings I take one daughter and my wife takes the other and we divide the list of chores. We each follow our list, but we spend the driving and shopping time with our daughters, making certain that we stop somewhere for lunch where the child will enjoy eating. (This usually means eating a burger and fries!) And we try to include an errand that the child chooses, like stopping at the toy store or feeding the ducks at the park.

Naturally, what would have taken maybe three hours to accomplish on my own takes twice as long with a child, but we have such a good time! Each kid loves it because it's a time to have either Mommy or Daddy all to herself. And the next week we switch kids. The girls are very enthusiastic about this; it really is a warm, uplifting time.

Ron: Bert, you have a unique situation because of your grandmother living with you. Does FATHERS help in that situation?

Bert: Absolutely. First of all, we welcomed Grandma with an attitude of being open about any problems. We agreed to expect difficulties and try to work them through before giving up. The first two weeks really were horrible. For some reason, my four-year-old son decided that he just didn't like Grandma. I found that we were constantly harping on Benjamin to stop being rude.

The other difficulty was that for my wife, it was like having a total stranger move into our home. FATHERS helped us learn to respect differences in personalities. We are all open with our feelings and we don't feel like we have to agree on every little thing in order to get along.

I try to relieve Kay of the extra work by insisting that she get out and have time for herself twice a week. She probably wouldn't do that if I didn't insist and she would wear herself down to a breaking point. Also, we learned in FATHERS how important it is for a woman to have her "conversation quota" filled each day. Both Kay and Grandma need to talk when I come home, so we spend a lot of time just sitting around talking about our day.

Ron: How did you work through the problem with Benjamin?

Bert: We arranged for Grandma to stay with other relatives for a long weekend. When she came back the situation was much better. Perhaps he needed to see that our family was still our family, with or without Grandma. Two weeks later Grandma went away again, this time for seven days. Benjamin actually said that he missed her, and was sincerely happy when she returned. It's so curious; I wish I knew what was going on in Benjamin's head.

Ron: What about your grandmother's feelings about living with the confusion and noise of three preschoolers?

Bert: We were concerned about that. But she always liked kids and she has her own room where she can close the door whenever she likes. She has a television of her own and other interests that keep her busy. There are at least a couple afternoons each week when the kids are out of the house. Lately, Grandma says the house is too quiet when the children aren't home.

Grandma has added a lot to our family. When she first came, our family held hands before supper and I prayed informally as usual. Grandma spoke right up and recited the rote prayer that she used all her life as a Roman Catholic. That's how we've continued—praying both ways every day. The kids now know the Catholic prayer and it's part of our worship.

One more thing. So many people comment, "Oh, I could never do that"—like it would be impossible to take in an elderly parent or that we are super Christians to bear this great burden. I'm really tired of hearing that. We aren't any kind of superspiritual martyrs. We've always been very free to say that if it doesn't work out, we'll find somewhere else for Grandma. It's that simple. But maybe hearing people say all the time, "Oh, I couldn't do that," makes us that much more determined to make it work.

Ron: George, what about the communication gap between teenagers and parents?

George: Our girls come home with all kinds of stories about things that happen to their friends at school. Parents who think they can hide their kids from anything these days are just fooling themselves. Things go on at school and it doesn't matter one bit what kind of school it is, public or private. The kids will talk it out at home if we let them. So we listen and we try hard not to act shocked! No matter what comes up, we try to keep an even keel and listen. Then we express our views in some way that will be honest but not judgmental.

If it seems that our daughter is taking the wrong standpoint, we offer additional information, like, "Before that person went and did such-and-such, do you think he considered these factors . . . ?" All these things are discussed at the dinner table and our nine-year-old listens to everything. You can only hope that your kids are bringing things home to you and not dealing with it someplace else.

Ron: David, you started us out with some really good thoughts. Do you have any comments to wind this up?

David: I need to admit that FATHERS hasn't always helped our family. I was halfway to the church one Monday morning when I realized I didn't have my Bible. I drove back to the house, only to discover that I had no key to get in. I had to pound on the window to wake Annie (this is about 5:45 A.M.). She heard me pound on the window so she got up and walked smack into the closet door that I'd left open. It took five days for the black eye and swelling to go down and she told everybody that it was due to my being in FATHERS. And since we learn in FATHERS to share everything with our spouses, she offered to get a Ping-Pong paddle and "share" a black eye with me! That was definitely not good for our family.

Ron: I think you have a misunderstanding, David, about the FATHERS intention to give a "shining" example to our wives—not a "shiner" example!

149

Prevention Is the Best

When you grow old, what are you going to remember? What will stand out as you think back on your family? Are you going to have fond memories or are you going to have frightful memories? Are you going to want to talk about your family or are you going to want to remain silent?

In this preventative kind of ministry, we have sought to pay the price now, because what you sow is what you reap. We want our children to reap good family experiences and memories.

As you think about your own family, maybe there are some memories that need to be healed. This kind of ministry is to get men turned around and to focus on the family. Again, it goes back to the thought that we are like sheep that have gone astray. Family times should be the most natural thing, yet it seems that family times are the most difficult and is the thing we are neglecting the most.

> For what is a man profited if he gains the whole world, and loses his own soul? Or what will a man give in exchange for his soul? (Matt. 16:26, *NKJV*).

And *I* would ask, what will it profit a man if he gains the whole world and loses his family?

Tips

Here are some helpful vacation tips:

State clearly at the onset of a trip exactly what behavior will and will not be tolerated in the car. There may come a time when you will need to stop the car and enforce the rules. The boys have known me to pull off the highway either to discipline them immediately or to let them know that I will not put up with certain things. That may seem severe, but it sets the tone for the family experience and we can all be more relaxed, knowing where the limits lie.

Involve children in planning vacations. Get out maps and let them plot the route, marking rest stops, picnic grounds and sights of interest along the way. Use calculators to figure mileage and costs and let the older children call motels to find the best rates, family plans and specials that may be offered—like pools, game rooms, guided nature hikes, etc.

Take mini-vacations to hotels in your own city or within a two-hour drive. Bring your own breakfast cereal, juice and doughnuts. Spend an afternoon at the pool, an hour in the game room and an evening watching TV and eating caramel corn together in bed.

When traveling with small children, plan ahead. The adult not driving keeps a "mystery bag" for each child. Do not let the child know what is in the bag and collect each toy or game before offering another. Be creative with the contents of your mystery bag:

- Fresh crayons or markers
- Booklets with invisible writing and "magic" pens
- Picture kits with rub-on decals
- Crossword puzzle books
- A View Master with new slides
- Nonmessy snacks
- Small jigsaw puzzle than can be worked in the car on a TV tray or flat box lid held on the lap.
- Tapes of children's songs, storybooks on cassette and talking books

- A tambourine to use when singing praise songs and camp tunes.

TAKING INVENTORY

1. Ask your family the following question: If money and time were not hindrances, what would you want to do during a weekend? Can some of their dreams become realities with a little planning, ingenuity and creativity?

2. Share with your family the times and experiences you have had together when you felt the closest. Ask each member to do likewise.

3. Reflect on some of the greatest disappointments your family has experienced. Analyze what went wrong. What could have prevented these disappointments? What future plans can be made to help offset the repeat of these disappointments?

4. Think of each person in your family. What can you do *with* or *for* him/her that will be a personal blessing?

5. Why is it important for a family to be together? Why is it important that family members have time away from each other?

6. What are your most treasured childhood memories? What can you share with your children? Why is it important to share childhood experiences?

7. What do you and your family do together that is truly enjoyed by everyone and often repeated?

8. How do you go about choosing your family fun times? Do even the small children have the opportunity to contribute their ideas?

Chapter 9

Spicing up Your Sex Life

*Even so husbands should love their wives
as their own bodies. He who loves his wife
loves himself. For no man ever hates his
own flesh, but nourishes and cherishes it,
as Christ does the church, because we are
members of his body. "For this reason a
man shall leave his father and mother
and be joined to his wife, and the two
shall become one." This is a great mystery, and I take it to mean Christ and the
church; however, let each one of you love
his wife as himself, and let the wife see
that she respects her husband (Eph. 5:28-
33).*

One of the greatest benefits in the FATHERS fellowship is the opportunity to talk with other men about personal matters. There is enormous relief in learning, "Hey, I'm not the only one with this problem!" In our squads and in our teachings, we have discovered the kind of trust relationships where we can be free to be open with each other, to learn and grow. I guess we've discussed just about every imaginable aspect of sexuality at one time or another, so this chapter is a *potpourri* of those ideas.

Members

The word MEMBERS is an acrostic to help keep ideas about sex in order:

> M—Mythical
> E—Educational
> M—Mental
> B—Biological
> E—Environmental
> R—Relational
> S—Spiritual

M—Mythical

I had difficulty settling on one word for the first *M*. We have been misinformed about sex, we have made serious mistakes, we have received misinstructions and we have misunderstood even the good instructions! Finally, I settled on the word *mythical* because it can be positive as well as negative.

In the field of theology a *myth* is a story that may be literally true, but also points to a reality greater than the visible. For example, the story of young George Washington chopping down the cherry tree may be based on fact, but the important point is the honest character of both the first

President and the nation he helped to establish. That story is an American myth. Using that *positive* meaning of myth, human sexuality expresses in a physical way the spiritual union of man and woman and the mystical union of Christ and His Church.

But the common meaning of myth is a misinterpretation of the truth. There are many negative myths about sex in the Christian Church today.

There is an attitude that sex is a spiritual gift that God gives to a couple on their wedding night; therefore, the Church doesn't need to teach about sex because it will all be revealed miraculously by the Holy Spirit on the wedding night. Sex is too sacred to talk about. Keep the young people in the dark and don't say anything!

Maybe I'm missing something, but frankly, I don't find sex in any of the New Testament lists of spiritual gifts. Of course I'm exaggerating, but this reflects much of the behavior and teaching (or lack of teaching) in today's Church. Sex is not a spiritual gift. Sex is a learned behavior and it may be learned badly, with disastrous results, or it may be learned well and developed through disciplined practice into a beautiful expression of love and commitment.

Jesus says in John 8:31-32,36: "If you continue in my word, you are truly my disciples, and you will know the truth, and the truth will make you free . . . . So if the Son makes you free, you will be free indeed." Jesus can set us free to be all that we were created to be. I believe we need to be set free from myth and misunderstanding.

Certainly we need to be set free from the myth that sex is not to be enjoyed. In the first centuries of Christianity some of the early fathers extolled celibacy and taught that marriage was permitted only because some believers were too weak to remain virgins. Other early authorities

157

disagreed by arguing from Scripture that Peter and most of the apostles were married and 1 Timothy teaches that a bishop is to be the husband of one wife. But celibacy was embraced by the Roman Church and the official position on sex swung back and forth through the centuries from being considered "a necessary evil" to "a blessing of God."

The Protestant Reformation recognized the goodness of married sex from the very beginning and continued to affirm married love through the Reformation. Ironically, the Puritans were blasted by the Catholic Church for lechery and lustful teachings because the Puritans taught that sex was a good creation of God and meant to be enjoyed! The Puritans were the scandal of their time.

In the latter part of the nineteenth century, popular medical theory declared that sex was unhealthy and ought to be avoided if at all possible. Thinking that the material world is evolving toward a higher spiritual realm, this idea had philosophical roots in Greek dualism, the separation of body and spirit, rather than in the biblical view of the goodness of creation. Sex was tolerated only as a repugnant necessity.

Even today, many difficulties in Christian marriages stem from that philosophy. If we think sex is only procreational, we fail to give ourselves permission to enjoy sex as God intended. Christ can set couples free from all the guilt and legalism of looking at sex as a necessary evil. Sex may *become* sin, like any other appetite. But sex as such is not sin.

At the opposite extreme we have the popular media claiming that it is unhealthy to repress any sexual impulse. Christians, they say, are Puritans who don't want anybody to have any fun! The Playboy philosophy promotes a male-oriented world, where women are objects to be used in any way for male gratification. Sex in the Playboy world is totally divorced from relationships, family, tenderness and affection. In the same vein, women and men crying for "liberation" have degraded sex to a mere biological function, stripped of responsibility and commitment.

Both males and females need to know that using any human being as an object for personal gratification is wrong. But sex is still *good!* Myths and misunderstandings will not change that fact. We need to know—really *know*—that God created sex to be an expression of spiritual union, deepest love and all of our deepest emotions. Besides all that, it's supposed to be fun!

E—Educational

Remember our FATHERS Oath? "I will receive the Word of God in my heart daily and will teach it diligently to my children . . . . " It seems obvious that we must know the Word before we can teach it to our children. "All Scripture is inspired by God to be used to teach the faith, for correcting error, setting us free from myth, setting direction for a man and woman's life and for training us in good living" (See 2 Tim. 3:16. This quote is from the Ron Rand version!). When we discover that truth, we may discover not only how to teach our children, but also how God can redeem sex in ourselves.

A Look at the Old Testament. Let's begin, then, with Genesis 2:24-25—the passage that speaks of leaving and cleaving and becoming one flesh. Sex is to be enjoyed lifelong by God's married children: those who have left their own parents and now cleave to one another. That word implies a permanent bonding, as when a branch is grafted onto another tree and the two grow permanently together. Notice that there is no mention of children in this passage.

Sex was created by God to be enjoyed, not just for procreation.

I have come to a greater understanding of this issue through going back and studying the passage in Hebrew. I've also studied the Greek Septuagint, trying to get a sense of what the ancient words really express. In the passage where the man says, "This at last is bone of my bones and flesh of my flesh" (v. 23), the basic idea is, "Whoopee! Where have you been all my life?" There is *joy* in the creation of sexual companionship and gratification in the Garden of Eden. And God says, "It is very good!"

Read Genesis 26:8. Isaac and Rebekah are living among the Philistines and Isaac has hidden the fact that Rebekah is his wife for fear of being killed. The king of the Philistines happens to see Isaac "fondling Rebekah his wife," and he knows immediately that this is no sister-brother relationship! There is no shame implied in their sexual fondling; that is assumed to be a natural aspect of the marriage relationship. Again, there is no mention of procreation.

Also read Deuteronomy 24:5. It says, When a man is newly married, he shall not go out with the army or be charged with any business; he shall be free at home one year, to be happy with his wife whom he has taken. "Happy" is an active verb meaning, "to have pleasure." That is, making her happy with sexual gratification. Again, it is notable that the text does not say that he is to stay at home in order to produce children. It is the sexual *pleasure* of the husband and wife that is to be protected.

I want to pay additional attention to an underlying principle in this text. The man and woman are to have time together, free from civic responsibilities, to enjoy one another. You see, it takes time to develop any kind of relationship, most especially the sexual relationship. Sexual technique is a skill that has to be learned in partnership with another person. I can't imagine anything more apt to be a dismal failure than the "one night stand"! No one expects to take up a paintbrush and create a masterpiece on the first canvas or write a symphony in the first effort. Why do people think that they can have great sex without working at it?

Right along with a lack of commitment goes the problem of performance expectation. When the emphasis is on having "great sex" rather than experiencing a "great relationship," it's just impossible to achieve lasting satisfaction. Sexual response is extremely difficult when there is the feeling that you are being graded or compared with other partners. Performance orientation is a real turnoff!

Again, it is always difficult to adjust to two different relationships at the same time, such as being newly married *and* going to school or starting a new job, etc. Whenever I counsel an engaged couple, I always inquire about their plans for that first year. If they are overloading themselves, I advise them to wait. Finish school first or give yourself two or three months to adjust at the new job *before* you step into marriage. The marriage will determine the course of the rest of their lives, so it is more than worthwhile to take the time to build a firm foundation, learn how to relate, focus on each other. What is one year of waiting compared to 50 years of married love?

Now read Proverbs 5:18-19, 21: "Let your fountain be blessed, and rejoice in the wife of your youth, a lovely hind, a graceful doe. Let her affection fill you at all times with delight, be infatuated always with her love . . . . For a man's ways are before the eyes of the LORD, and he watches all his paths."

This passage is a clear description of sexual intercourse between man and wife. Certain scholars suggest that the hind and doe were used as examples because those creatures have the most urgent and passionate mating behavior. There is no suggestion in this passage that sex is an unpleasant necessity to produce children. Children are never mentioned, but look at what it *does* say: "Be blessed . . . delight . . . be infatuated always." And all this sexual behavior is good "before the eyes of the Lord."

Sex therapists say that a person enters an altered state of consciousness during sexual arousal. This mental state is contrasted with normal consciousness of daily activities such as reading, conversation, driving a car, etc. Other altered states include sleeping and dreaming or times when one is overwhelmed with grace from the Lord. Chemically-induced altered states might be very positive, as in the use of anesthesia, or negative, as in the abuse of drugs or alcohol.

Many individuals resist entering into the sexual experience because it seems so strange. They think, "That's not me. I turn into something else. I'm out of control." Many men dislike their sexual lives because they feel shame. Many women experience the same confusion, fearing their own responses or their spouse who "isn't himself."

Proverbs 5:19 describes this altered state of consciousness in sexuality when it says, "Be infatuated always with her love." This is good in the eyes of the Lord, as spouses are intended to have their minds and spirits in tune with one another. Understanding that this is a natural, desirable response may reassure and prepare couples to respond joyfully as husband and wife.

Proverbs 18:22 is another good reference. It says, "He who finds a [spouse] finds a good thing, and obtains favor from the LORD." Again and again, it is clear that sex within marriage is a blessing of God.

How did the Song of Solomon get into the Bible? It

looks like a manual on married love and sex in poetic form! That is exactly what it is. God created sex and the Christians who discerned the books that were to be included in the Canon recognized God's goodness in the totality of creation. This text includes a man's description of his wife's body, including her sexual parts, and his praises to God for the beautiful creature that she is. The woman also describes her husband's body from head to toe and includes praises to God for the wonderful creature *he* is. Both husband and wife express their passionate desires for one another, in the beauty and privacy of the marriage bed.

A Look at the New Testament. Moving to the New Testament, I just want to focus on two passages in 1 Corinthians, beginning with chapter 7:1-9. Our English translations are awkward and I suspect that this reflects the bias of various translators. For example, where the *Revised Standard* version uses, "give . . . conjugal rights" (v. 3), the *King James* version says, "render . . . due benevolence" and the Living paraphrase says, "give . . . all that is her right as a married woman." Paul is trying to say that both the husband and wife have the right to sexual gratification in marriage. Notice that the man and woman are equal in their rights to have sex with their spouse. The Scriptures recognize that the sexual needs of both women and men are definite, pronounced and given by God. It is good for a woman to take the initiative to express her desire for sex, just as it is good for the man to take the initiative. Both are responsible to continually meet one another's needs. As in every other area of the Christian life, each spouse is always to put the other's desire or need ahead of one's own.

In verse 5, sexual intercourse is assumed to be a natural function of marriage. It is extraordinary to abstain from sex. Abstention is strictly limited to a period of fasting (for prayer and, we might safely assume, for medical reasons when necessary). Then we are specifically told to come together for sex again. What could be more plain and simple than this direct recognition of pleasure and passion?

The other passage I want to point out is found in verse 14 of the same chapter. It is clear to me here that children need to be brought up in a good healthy marriage where there is a good healthy attitude toward sex. I believe that children should learn about sex in the home. Too often, children learn about sex through the Hollywood version presented in films, television and popular music. Is it any wonder that we see tragic Hollywood-type divorces replayed in those children as they grow up and practice what they observe?

The Church's goal must be to equip and encourage parents to train up children in the way they should go. But in the area of sex, the Church has committed the sin of omission in failing to either teach parents how to teach children or to teach the children directly.

M—Mental
I was thinking about this section of the book while flying to a conference in Pennsylvania when suddenly an announcement broke into my thoughts: "We are preparing to land in North Umberland, Pennsylvania. Please fasten your seat belts. All luggage must be secured under the seats, all cigarettes must be extinguished and all seats must be placed in the upright position."

The pilot was preparing the plane and the passengers for landing using specific instructions. In the same way, we need to prepare our minds for experiencing sex.

How does your wife think about herself? Does she complain about being too fat? Does she think her hips are too big or her bust too small? Does she feel like a frumpy housewife? What can you do to make her think of herself as desirable? Have you read passages from Song of Solomon to her? They declare, "Behold, you are beautiful, my love . . . . I will hie me to the mountain of myrrh and the hill of frankincense. O queenly maiden! Your rounded thighs are like jewels, the work of a master hand . . . your belly is a heap of wheat, encircled with lilies. Your two breasts are like two fawns . . . " (Song of Sol. 1:15; 4:6; 7:1-3). This was no Skinny Minnie that captured Solomon in her tresses! When your wife knows that she is physically desirable in *your eyes,* she will be mentally and emotionally prepared to take delight in physical love.

The wife likewise ought to encourage her husband with positive thoughts about himself and prepare him for sex by courtship and flirtation. This is important, for it is okay for a woman to enjoy sex and to take the initiative. Even in this age of "liberation," the image of the "pure and innocent little girl" is so deeply imbedded in many of our young women that wives find it difficult to express sexual impulses. Even after years of marriage, a wife may be embarrassed about her physical urges. As husbands, we need to give our wives "permission" to be sexual. How will a woman know that her husband really gets turned on when she's aggressive if he doesn't tell her?

One couple had planned an evening of sexual intimacy, but during the afternoon the wife was upset by a misunderstanding with a friend and felt under great strain all evening. The husband understood and said, "Let's not be bound to our plans for intimacy tonight in light of what's happened. I feel tender toward you because I sense your hurt and I'd just like to hold you tonight, without any sexual expectations."

So his wife was comforted and they were able to just

be together and feel close to one another that evening. From that experience, however, came three beautifully intimate times later in the week because the woman knew that she was understood, cared for and loved—apart from performance expectations.

All of the emotions of the day help to determine a spouse's readiness for a sexual experience. The husband who ignores his wife all day and expects a great performance in the bedroom is going to be disappointed!

B—Biological

Most sex manuals concentrate on the physiological aspects of sex: necking, petting, various lovemaking techniques, etc., and these are all useful. But we often overlook the obvious: fatigue or illness, a cold or allergy, age or obesity or disabilities. These are all important factors in sexual performance. Physical difficulties may stem from something as simple as needing time in the evening together to become mentally ready for sex. (You don't have to explain *why* you are dropping off the board of deacons!) Or it may be that a recent bout with the flu has left one spouse drained and without interest in sex for several days. In these cases, we need to keep the lines of communication open to protect one another from misunderstandings and needless blame.

On the other hand, such factors may be used as excuses when some other problem has not been properly resolved. If a wife's mental attitude has not been prepared, she may claim to have a headache to avoid sex. Or a man may come home and claim to be too tired for sex, when the real problem may be resentment or unforgiveness. Constant avoidance of sex is a signal of a problem that needs correction.

Whenever there is a physical problem such as impotence, painful intercourse or infections, the couple should seek immediate medical help. One young bride was terrified shortly after her honeymoon when she developed a vaginal yeast infection. The only thing she could think of was venereal disease and she didn't know what to think or say to her husband! The pain became so intense that she rushed to the doctor, who calmly reassured her that she had a yeast infection that is as common as a cold. A change of soap and instructions on cleanliness for both spouses corrected the problem.

Getting Specific. Since this is a book written especially for fathers, I will focus on the men. A great majority of sexual difficulties can be corrected if we will remember to proceed slowly in sex until the wife is ready—no, eager—before proceeding. Some FATHERS members have shared about developing particular patterns in lovemaking: talking and laughing about the day, rubbing backs, talking about emotions, cuddling, petting. Some have discovered that a particular type of rubbing or stroking is necessary for arousal and that the pattern may change from time to time.

One key to success is for each spouse to tell one another what feels good and what doesn't: what tickles, what itches, what is hot or cold or wild or icky. It also includes whispering what she's always imagined she might like to do or hinting at a silly little idea that maybe he might try. If you give your spouse permission to try things, to experiment, to tell you what she likes, then lovemaking can blossom and grow beyond all your dreams.

"Wait a minute," you caution. "Is all this experimenting proper?" Absolutely! Read Hebrews 13:4 *(KJV)*: "Marriage is honourable in all, and the bed undefiled." No Scripture defines certain positions or actions as proper between husband and wife. All physical expressions of love and passion that give pleasure to both spouses and that cause no injury are good. Again, communication is critical. If something hurts or if one partner would rather not experiment in a certain way, the other spouse must consider the partner's needs above his or her own desires. But there is no scriptural limit to lovemaking!

Remember, the key to a good relationship is constant communication as to what is desirable and pleasurable. Most of us need reassurance that it is okay to talk about feelings, touching and intimacy.

A child primarily receives his sexual identity from the parent of the opposite sex. Therefore, it is important for a mother to convey approval and warmth to her sons. It is equally necessary for a father to give approval and affection to his daughters.

E—Environmental

The best environment for intimacy includes privacy, comfort and seclusion from interruption or distractions. Other elements vary according to individual preferences. One FATHERS member told of going camping specifically to be alone with his wife. Out in the wilderness with the sound of an owl, a lapping lake and moonlight through the trees—what could be more romantic! He hadn't considered strange sounds in the dark, the hard ground and those twigs and tiny stones that kept poking through the canvas floor of the tent! There was very little romance that weekend!

Another FATHERS member likes to have lots of candles lit so he can see his beloved by candlelight. But his beloved prefers romancing in total darkness. Invariably, as soon as he has lit all the candles and has snuggled under the blanket, his wife will jump out of bed and blow the candles out!

Other personal preferences may include temperature, the number of blankets, silence, background music and even odor. A FATHERS member (who will remain anonymous!) discovered that his wife became much more friendly when he remembered to leave his smelly shoes outside their bedroom door!

Privacy is a more serious environmental matter. A lock on the bedroom door or firmly teaching the kids to respect a closed door is essential.

Still, the inevitable does happen. How do you respond to the child who accidently breaks in on you? Most children will need assurance that Daddy is not hurting Mommy and this is something that married people do that is good, but is only for husbands and wives. Depending on the age of the child, reassurance that this is a natural, good activity may be sufficient. For older children, the experience can be followed (the next day, perhaps) with further teaching on sexuality and God's plan for building families. Try to turn what might be a frightening situation into a beautiful opportunity for learning.

R—Relational

The relational aspect of sexuality is important. If we think of our spouse as an object for our personal gratification, sex will suffer.

Lust is when you're there for the sensation instead of the unification. Lust is a turnoff and is harmful to relationships because it seems as though the partner is interested in selfish gratification instead of tender expressions of affection. Lust is ugly to see in a husband or wife.

Clinically, lust may be defined as "the desire for repetition of remembered erotic pleasure: the way it felt last week." It is wanting an instant replay of feelings experienced in another time and place—and maybe even with another person.

Lust can be observed in other aspects of life, even in prayer life. Maybe I remember a particular Easter Sunday when I was touched by the Lord and had an ecstatic experience. Wow! I want that experience again! So I go to the same sanctuary, sing the same songs, pray the same prayer and wait to feel what I felt before. That is lust.

God does not provide reruns of last year's religious experiences. God is living and His work is new every morning. I am different today from what I was yesterday and my spiritual experience must be unique to today. And what is true in my relationship with God must be true in my relationship with my spouse. "This is the day which the LORD has made; let us rejoice and be glad in it" Ps. 118:24).

The key is to have our priorities in the right order. Desire for a remembered experience will *prevent* a new experience, but sincere uniting of spirit and heart in love for one another will blossom into the desired sensation.

As in other areas of the FATHERS Ministry, we learn to see the wife as a partner. We have to be certain that the relationship is right before approaching lovemaking: being certain there are no unfulfilled promises, mistaken expectations or forgotten responsibilities. When there is no bitterness between us, our love will be sweet. According to the principle in Matthew 5:23-24, if the husband realizes that he has offended his wife, he must go immediately to ask her forgiveness. Also, in Matthew 18:15, if a wife has been wounded, she should go to her husband and clear the matter up promptly, and vice versa. Read 2 Corinthians 5:17-21. God is the reconciler, willing that we should be in right relationships.

Confusion over the possibility of pregnancy can interfere with a good, relaxed sexual relationship. The act of intercourse may take only 20 minutes, but it could result in nine months of pregnancy, eight months of nursing, six years of intimate care and many, many more years of responsibility for another life—not to mention the financial commitment. The reality and possibility of pregnancy will color the way both partners think and feel about sex. The type of contraception used must be comfortable, safe and a method acceptable to both spouses.

Jesus can free us from cultural expectations and this also relates to procreation. Among some groups, the popular thinking is to have no more than one or two children. Others believe adoption is better than having any children at all. This standard may relate less to ecological ideals than to the fact that children interfere with self-centered life-styles.

Other communities expect religious families to have "as many children as the Lord will give," regardless of medical problems or emotional and financial stresses. Again, such standards are primarily cultural expectations.

I do not advocate irresponsibility in any way, but I urge couples to seek the Lord for His guidance in His individual will for them. There is wisdom in seeking advice from parents and elders, as well as from medical professionals regarding any physical complications. God does not have one "perfect will" in procreation that applies to all Christian marriages.

S—Spiritual

The culmination then, is the mysterious truth that the husband and wife are joined in a spiritual relationship. We have come full circle and are back to sex as a *myth* in the positive sense: a beautiful mystery representing a truth above and beyond the visible reality.

My first exposure to the realities of the opposite sex occurred when I was in junior high. A friend that I admired very much gave me a "girlie book." (I thought that was pretty strong stuff, back in 1954, but by today's standards it was mild indeed!) I brought the magazine home and stuck it under my mattress. The next day when I came home from school, lifted up the mattress and began to feel around, I discovered that the magazine was gone!

It was a very quiet supper that night and I thought maybe it was my last. At the end of the meal my father announced that he wanted to see me in my room. He followed me carrying not my girlie magazine, but his medical books. And I had a crash course on human anatomy. As soon as he was done in came my mother and she gave a crash course on human relationships from a woman's point of view. As soon as that course was completed in came my sister, who gave me a crash course on sociology and psychology from a girl's point of view. That was one lesson I could really understand, coming from a peer.

So in that one evening, with all of those crash courses, I became an "expert" on the physical, emotional and mental aspects of sex. But there was one thing that I lacked: the understanding that I was a creation of God and He had created those desires in me. I lacked insight into the spiritual aspect of sexuality.

Although 1 Corinthians 6:13-20 deals with a man joined with a prostitute, we can develop the positive understanding that a man's spirit will be intwined with the spirit of his wife and the wife's spirit with her husband's. There is something of the Spirit that is a mystery when transmitted together with the biological experience. In the intimate intertwining of our lives and in the loving bond that transcends the physical experience, God has revealed something of Himself to those whom He has called.

And It Was Good

Jesus became flesh and dwelt among us, full of grace and truth. As FATHERS members we make a firm commitment to renew the totality of our whole being and to allow Jesus to fill our own flesh with grace and truth. This is a commitment to share our deepest selves with our wives in a clear relationship in the eyes of the Lord Jesus Christ. We claim sex as part of His good creation and view it as a blending of complex and constantly varying factors which can work together or conflict with one another to produce a variety of sexual responses. Myths, education, the mind, biology, environment, our relationships and the Spirit—all these are the ingredients, mixed together, that form the kind of union the Lord in His creation described as good.

Tips

Take advantage of weekend or off-season specials at hotels to have an annual or semiannual honeymoon. Make time for special communication involving the mental, emotional and physical aspects of your relationship. Look back over your life together and set goals for the future.

Romancing this evening? Make certain that the telephone is unplugged.

Variety is the Spice of Life. Consider adding some spice to your love life by incorporating the following ideas:

1. Arrange to make love in the morning or afternoon before the kids get home from school. Room-darkening shades can be purchased and remember, love doesn't only flourish at night!

173

2. Consider trying different positions for intercourse. Discuss this with your mate and explore together. Give yourself permission to laugh at your inexperience. Remember, practice makes perfect.

One Good Turn Deserves Another. Arrange with another couple who also have children to turn over your kids to them for an evening so you and your wife can have a time alone together in your own home. Return the favor to that couple. This is an inexpensive way of being together, as well as a wonderful way of developing other family ties.

TAKING INVENTORY

1. Evaluate the following areas of intimacy with your mate. Which area is your strongest? Which area needs growth? What are you willing to change or do for this growth to occur?
   a. Sharing of interests (athletics, hobbies, entertainment, travel).
   b. Sharing of emotions and personal feelings (all those times when you use personal pronouns: "*I* feel . . . . ").
   c. Sharing of spiritual things (prayer, worship, fellowship).
   d. Sharing of bodies (touching, hugging, back rubbing, petting, sexual intercourse).

2. Discuss with your mate what each of you consider the ideal lovemaking situations.

3. Discuss what one partner should do when he/she wants to make love and the spouse does not.

4. What circumstances put your wife in the mood for love? What circumstances put you in the mood for love?

5. Can you schedule sex? Why or why not?

6. Are you doing the things that let your wife know she is loved? For example, are you performing the chores around the house?

7. Are you seeking to communicate effectively with your wife? Are you able to talk about your sex life? How and when can such conversations occur?

8. Have you and your wife gone on a date recently? Describe your last date.

9. Are there some areas of unresolved conflict between you and your wife? Identify them and approach those areas one at a time. What Scripture is helpful to you?

10. Are you groomed as well as your wife wants you to be?

11. Do you ever have sex in different settings at home or away? Identify some areas and consider them in the future.

12. Comment on how well you believe you listen to your wife. Do you understand both her feelings *and* the factual content of what she says? Are you giving her your full attention? Analyze your body language. What is the message you are giving?

Chapter 10

Leading Your Children to Christ

Every one who believes that Jesus is the Christ is a child of God, and every one who loves the parent loves the child. By this we know that we love the children of God, when we love God and obey his commandments (1 John 5:1-2).

I see a great need in the Christian community for parents, and fathers in particular, to learn how to bring their children to a saving knowledge of Jesus Christ.

We seem to expect kids to get their religious experiences outside of the home, at youth groups or choir or at Christian summer camp. I see parents bringing their kids to Sunday Church School, expecting those teachers to give their children a solid Bible foundation. Kids are expected to "get religion" by osmosis: simply by sitting beside us in the worship service or, at the very least, in the communicant's classes. Of course those things are good. But by themselves, these things are not enough.

We've moved away from the Old Testament understanding that religious training is to take place in the home.

Very few parents know how to lead children to Christ. Children need their parents to intentionally train them to pray, how to deal with temptation and to defend one another.

> Hear, O Israel: The LORD our God is one LORD; and you shall love the LORD your God with all your heart, and with all your soul, and with all your might. And these words which I command you this day shall be upon your heart; and you shall teach them diligently to your children, and shall talk of them when you sit in your house, and when you walk by the way, and when you lie down, and when you rise. And you shall bind them as a sign upon your hand, and they shall be as frontlets between your eyes. And you shall write them on the doorposts of your house and on your gates (Deut. 6:4-9).

How is this passage acted out in our homes? Well, let's look at my house. There is an *ichthus* fish over the mailbox and door knocker that reads, "Peace to All Who Enter Here." I don't know how many little plaques and samplers and little slogans there are all around the house with phrases and passages of Scripture on them.

Maybe your house is the same. Actually, it would be very difficult in any part of our house—from the front porch to the bathroom—not to notice that religious people live here!

Then there is the "testimony-to-go": I often wear a fish pin on my jacket, Jennifer has a beautiful cross necklace and our boys have lots of T-shirts with mottos such as, "Grow in the Family of God" or "Christian Under Construction." Someone even gave me a sweatband that says "Jogging for Jesus." (I haven't appeared in public wearing that one yet!)

This kind of witness is okay for encouragement and fun, but if we think it fulfills Deuteronomy 6, we've missed the point. Verse 7 says that we must *teach* the ways of God diligently to our children—that we shall talk of them when we sit, when we walk (jog?), when we lie down and when we rise." That means more than grace at meals and "Now I lay me down to sleep . . . " at bedtime.

Faith of the Fathers

Nevertheless, my number one responsibility is to evangelize my own children. In the words of my dad, everything else appears "pale and washed out" when compared with that fervent desire.[1]

A close friend of mine, who is also a Presbyterian minister, tells of an evening when a visiting evangelist had come to hold a series of services at his church. Joel was sitting in the congregation with his son, Joel Jr. When an invitation to come forward to accept Jesus as personal Saviour was given at the end of the sermon, his son indicated that he wanted to respond. Joel sort of discouraged him, thinking that his response was due to the emotional nature of the call rather than a moving of the Holy Spirit. After all, Presbyterians don't do this sort of thing very often and he felt that maybe his son didn't have the proper objective in the situation.

But Joel Jr. became more and more insistent and finally Joel said, "Okay, go on up." As he watched his boy hurry up the aisle, this father saw his two teenaged daughters joining their brother by kneeling together at the altar. Now, that must have been some experience for Joel, as he saw his three children make their personal commitments to Jesus Christ together!

Joel told me of this experience just after I had spent a week studying and designing methods of helping parents explain salvation to their children. It convinced me that I was on the right track. My friend Joel who earned a Doctor of Ministry degree, has brought scores of individuals to a saving knowledge of Jesus Christ. He and his wife have raised those kids in a solid Christian home from day one. Yet he was not the final link in bringing his children to Christ. It happened (1) outside the home; (2) in the church; (3) at a special evangelistic service and (4) with a visiting pastor.

It's time for Christian men to come to grips with the fact that they are responsible for nurturing their own children in the faith. The Church as an educational institution is only supplemental to what should be happening in the home. I believe we ought to hear more testimonies from people who say, "I came to know Christ through my parents" rather than, "I heard about Christ through Billy Graham," (or Campus Crusade or whatever). We rarely hear early testimonies such as, "I can't remember when I wasn't a Christian because my parents taught me from early childhood to know Jesus."

Bringing our own children up in the nurture and knowledge of the Lord takes a lot of effort and a lot of time.

Joshua became a Christian on August 12, 1974. He and I were digging in our backyard and we came across a plastic bead, like a pearl. He began asking me questions about God and as we talked, he expressed a desire to pray and invite Jesus into his heart. We kept that plastic pearl to represent the "pearl of great price" that he found that day.

Nathan became a Christian on May 23, 1977. I had been at an evangelism clinic in Michigan and he asked me what I had been doing. I told him I was teaching people about Jesus and how they can know Him personally and invite Him into their lives. He said, "I want to invite Jesus into my life," and he did so, sitting with me on our love seat. He identifies that little couch as the place where he began his spiritual life.

Nathan led Christopher to Christ sometime close to Christmas one year—which is also Christopher's natural birthday. So Christmas is a special time for Christopher and our family in three ways: it is Jesus' birthday, Christopher's natural birthday and Christopher's spiritual birthday!

When these anniversaries come around each year, I like to take the "birthday" child into the sanctuary at the church when it is empty and place candles in the large candlesticks there. One candle represents each year of his Christian life. We light the candles and pray a special prayer of thanksgiving for the new and never fading life that God has given us.

Hard Questions

In 1956, when I first shared my personal commitment to Jesus Christ with my parents, I asked them a simple question: "Mom and Dad, why weren't you the ones who asked me to accept Jesus Christ as my personal Saviour and Lord? I mean, it would have been so natural, because all my life I've seen Jesus Christ in your lives. I know He lives because I have seen Him alive in you. So why weren't *you* the ones who actually showed me *how* to receive Him into my life?"

Though the question was simple, the answer my father gave was profound. With tears in his eyes and after a glance at Mom, whose eyes were also teary, he said, "Son, we've assumed too much, we've assumed too much."

I wonder how many Christian parents, family members or indeed pastors have assumed that those growing up in Christian homes are automatically involved in a personal relationship with Jesus Christ. It's as if Christianity—a personal faith relationship—is thought by some to be developed by osmosis or passed from one family member to another like a virus!

My main concern in this chapter is to encourage you and your family members to be prepared to lead your immediate and extended family members, and young children in particular, to a personal commitment to Jesus Christ. This is the most important objective in the world—all else is hay and stubble.

I shared with a group of pastors that conversation I had with my parents. After my talk, we paused for the evening meal and one of the elders approached me and asked if he might speak with me. "You know that story you told about you and your parents? Well, that's been true about me concerning my kids." At this point tears began welling up in his eyes. "I went home for supper just now and asked our 11-year-old son if he knew Jesus personally or just knew a lot of stuff about Him. He said that he just knew stuff, he didn't *know* Jesus." At this point my brother in Christ broke down and sobbed out loud. "I led my boy to invite Jesus into his life tonight. I want to thank you and thank God for opening my eyes to what was happening in my own home. I feel closer to my son now than I've ever felt before."

Basic Guidelines

For everything there is a season, and a time for
every matter under heaven (Eccles. 3:1).

I believe this verse is especially true when asking children to accept Jesus Christ by faith as their own Saviour
and to know Him as Lord of their lives. For each child
there is a time: there is a time to share and a time to
refrain from sharing. My prayer is always twofold:

1. That every parent will diligently wait upon
   the Lord to reveal the actual time to share
   with each child how he or she can personally
   respond to accepting Jesus Christ.
2. That every parent will reverence Christ as
   Lord in their heart and "always be prepared
   to make a defense to any [child] who calls
   you to account for the hope that is in you,
   yet do it with gentleness and reverence" (1
   Pet. 3:15).

My prayer is that the various approaches and ideas
that I describe here will be a source of encouragement and
a means of releasing God's grace into your family. Please
do not misunderstand me by thinking that the examples I
give in this chapter need to be followed word-for-word.
Always adapt any presentation to the child or children
present, according to the visual aids on hand and according
to the leading of the Holy Spirit at the moment.

Although you should do your best to work in a manner
that is theologically correct, it is ultimately the Holy Spirit
who brings individuals into His family—not the skill of the
presenter or the accuracy of the presentation.

> But to all who received him, who believed in his
> name, he gave power to become children of
> God; who were born, not of blood nor of the will
> of the flesh nor of the will of man, but of God
> (John 1:12-13).

I realize that all of the illustrations and accompanying theology may not reflect a strict reformed theology. That is just as well, as the methods here are intended to be applicable in any denominational setting. And I have confidence that the Holy Spirit will honor our efforts. In saying this, I do not mean to suggest a cheap grace. Jesus Christ is the Way, the Truth and the Life. I trust in Him to straighten out any of the kinks in the methodology and to perfectly conform to His image those who receive Him and who believe in His name.

Essential Ingredients

The pivotal question must be, What needs to be contained in a basic gospel message directed toward children? Must it necessarily contain the doctrine of sin or can it reflect the essence of Jesus' teaching on children? According to Johannine texts, a child's simple trust is counted as faith and all who receive Him and believe in His name will receive power to become His children. Can not the years that follow a child's initial introduction to Jesus be used by the Holy Spirit to teach and enlighten the child of various aspects of sin and separation, building on the reality of grace?

> Without faith it is impossible to please him. For
> whoever would draw near to God must believe
> that he exists and that he rewards those who
> seek him (Heb. 11:6).

Paul's teaching from 1 Corinthians 2:15-16 also indicates that those who possess the Spirit within them can understand spiritual truths. Jesus says the same in His discourse with Nicodemus. Could it be, therefore, that the essential element in the gospel is receiving the Spirit, the Counselor, the One who imparts understanding of spiritual truths? I believe that it is.

These are the general guidelines I follow when attempting to communicate the gospel to children:

1. Get on the child's level by getting down on your knees, sitting on a low chair or curling up on the floor.

2. Eye contact is essential because it tells the child that you are personally interested in him or her.

3. Smile and communicate with bright, cheerful expressions. Remember, this is the Good News.

4. Use language and concepts appropriate for the age of the child.

5. Repeat every point using a variety of words and examples. Repetition aids retention.

6. Use a visual aid whenever possible because children think in the concrete, rather than in the abstract.

7. Explain how *you* first came to a personal relationship with Jesus Christ. Be brief.

8. Give an opportunity for the child to pray in his/her own words. If this is not possible, lead the child in a simple prayer in which

he/she repeats each phrase after you.

9. After the prayer of commitment, pray for the child using Matthew 19:13-14 as a guide.

10. Review with the child what has been said and what occurred through the prayer of commitment.

11. Record this special time with a photograph or some memory token.

12. If you are acting as a teacher or youth leader, contact the child personally within the following week to reinforce the commitment. Moms and Dads can make a practice of reinforcement for the first several days.

13. Parents, commit yourself to pray continually for and with your child. Pray over your sleeping child at night before you retire. God's indwelling Spirit is conscious while the child's spirit is unconscious.

14. Encourage the child to memorize an appropriate Bible verse (that you might paraphrase) to help communicate what has happened. Try to use the child's name in the verse in place of the pronouns:

For God so loved (Rebekah) that he gave his only Son, that as (Rebekah) believes in him, (Rebekah) will not perish but have eternal life (John 3:16).

Notice that I added the child's name for "the world" and "whoever," repeated the name a third time and replaced the "should," found in the *Revised Standard Ver-*

sion, to the more commonly used, "will." This emphasizes the certainty indicated in the text. I am of the opinion that while textual accuracy is essential to theology, the priority in personal witnessing must be the effective communication of the textual *content*—God's personal love.

Other verses I have found useful are:

Psalm 23:1-6	2 Corinthians 5:17
John 1:12	1 John 5:11-12
Romans 10:9-10,13	Revelation 3:20

In the following illustrations I will assume that you are a parent or family member presenting the Good News. Any reference to a "helper" indicates a pastor, teacher or layperson.

Spiritual Breathing

> *Verse to memorize:* "He breathed on (name) and said, '(name), receive the Holy Spirit'" (see John 20:22).

This is the method I used when three-year-old Joshua came to Christ as we worked in the backyard one afternoon. He began by asking some difficult questions involving where God lived, heaven and how God could fit in people's hearts. This scripted monologue closely resembles my explanation to Joshua.

Where does God live? Yes, God lives in
heaven, but also someplace else. Can you guess

187

where else God lives? (Receive each answer with affirmation.)

God lives in heaven, but He also lives in the hearts of everyone who asks Him to come into their hearts.

Where is your heart? Can you tell me? Yes, inside your body. How can God come and live inside of your heart?

Jesus said that God's Spirit is like the wind. In fact, the Bible uses the same word for Spirit as for wind.

Let me ask you to blow on your hand. Can you do that? Okay, now do it again, but this time as you blow on your hand, try to see the wind that comes from your mouth. Did you see it? Of course not. We can't see the wind with our eyes, but we can feel it on our hands.

God's Spirit is like the wind. We can't see Him with our eyes, but He is as real as the wind. We can't see the wind, we can only see what the wind does.

Now, I have a question for you. Where did the wind come from when you blew on your hand? It came from your lungs, which are inside your body, right? How did the air get into your body? Yes, by breathing. Take a breath right now. Okay, did you let the air in? (Child answers yes.) *Did you actually see the air go in?* (Child answers no.) *We can't see the air, but it is there, isn't it? But look what happens to your chest when you breathe the air. Your chest moves and gets bigger. The air you breathe does that.*

So is there air inside of you? (Child answers

yes.) *And there is air out here, blowing around
making wind, right? And there is air way up in
the sky and in the clouds where the birds and
airplanes fly, right?*

*God is like the air and like the wind. God is
in heaven and God is everywhere. And God will
come inside of your heart, if you invite Him in.
Would you like to invite God to come to live in
your heart now?*

The Spiritual Balloon

A related approach uses a balloon to illustrate that air is
invisible, yet has the power to change visible things. It will
provide a concrete example and the child can keep the
balloon as a reminder of this conversation. Begin by
showing the child a deflated balloon.

*Will the balloon get blown up by itself,
without any air in it?* (No, it won't.) *If I want
this balloon to have air in it, I have to blow air
into it, right? Just like this.* (Blow it up.) *Now,
there is air inside of it, right? Can you see the
air in it? No, but we can see that the air
changes the balloon, doesn't it?*

*God is like the wind or the air. We can't see
Him, but He is real. He wants to come to live
inside our hearts, but He won't come in unless
we want Him to and ask Him to do so. I
remember when I first asked God into my life.*
(Share a *brief* personal testimony. Remember,
small children have a limited attention span!)

*Would you like to let God's Spirit come into
your heart? You can do it by simply wanting
Him to come in and asking Him to come in. Do*

you want Him to come into your heart? Would
you like to ask Him to come into your heart right
now? Okay, why don't you talk to God right now
and tell Him you want Him to come into your
heart. Then ask Him to do so. Can you do that
in your own words?

After the prayer, read Matthew 19:13-14:

Then children were brought to (Jesus) that he
might lay his hands on them and pray. The
disciples rebuked the people; but Jesus said,
"Let the children come to me, and do not hinder
them; for to such belongs the kingdom of
heaven."

Explain that you want to put your hands on him or her
and pray as Jesus did. Ask the child if this is okay. If
agreed, lay your hands gently on the child's shoulders or
head and pray, thanking God for the child (by name) and
for this particular time in the child's life. Pray that God
will:

- Seal this decision
- Continue to help the child understand what He has
  done
- Bless the child with a sense of being a beloved
  child with whom God is well pleased.

When this prayer is completed, blow up the balloon
and tie the end in a knot. Explain that this balloon is a
symbol of what has been done in this time of prayer. Just
as the air is now in the balloon, so God's Spirit is in the
child's heart.

Explain that you have tied the balloon to keep the air inside. In the same way, the prayer is a way of sealing or keeping God's Spirit inside our hearts. The air will leak out of the balloon in a couple of days, but God will never leave the child's heart. Give the balloon to the child as a sign of the child's decision. Bring the balloon to the table during the evening meal and celebrate with the whole family what has taken place or suggest that the child share his or her experience, using the balloon as an example.

Tied Together

> *Verse to memorize:* "For God so loved the world that he gave his only Son, that whoever believes in him should not perish but have eternal life" (John 3:16).

This approach is effective when addressing a group of young children, perhaps those in kindergarten through second grade.

How many of you can tie your own shoelaces? Good! We take the two laces and tie them together like this, right? Okay. Now I can walk (stand up and walk in place) *and my shoes won't fall off. That's good! Shoelaces are supposed to be tied together* (sit down again).

But what happens if my shoelace comes untied? My shoe might fall off or I might trip and fall down. (Affirm every answer.) *Okay, if my shoelaces are untied, things don't work right. My shoe might fall off or I might trip and hurt myself.*

Our relationship with God is something like a shoelace. When God first created people, the relationship worked because everything was together. But the first people sinned—they chose to disobey God—and their relationship was broken like this shoelace coming untied.

Sometimes we speak of sin as "falling into sin." There is a verse in the Bible that says, "All have sinned and fallen short of the glory of God." So just as we fall down when our shoe is untied, people fall into sin when their relationship with God comes apart.

But God didn't just give up and let us stumble around, falling down and hurting ourselves and each other. Another verse in the Bible tells what He did:

For God so loved everyone in the world that He sent His only Son, that whosoever believes in Him should not be separated (die) but have life forever and ever. (See John 3:16.)

God's Son, Jesus, came to bring us back together with God.

Now, look at my shoelaces again. They are all untied, hanging loose. How do I get them back together again? I have to tie them, that's right. They won't tie themselves. Do you believe that I can tie them together again? Okay, let's see if I can. (Tie shoelaces.) There.

You said that you believed I could join these two laces together and I did. Do you believe in Jesus, that He can join us with God forever?

But what do I mean when I say, "Believe in

*Jesus?" It is not to pretend that He can do this,
but to say that for sure, He does. It is to say that
He really does join us with God forever and that
it is true and not pretend.*

*Would you like to tell Jesus you believe that?
Would you like to say a prayer and ask Jesus to
join you together with God? Okay, let's pray.
Remember, prayer is simply talking with God,
just like we are talking to one another right
now. Can you talk to Jesus in your own words
and thank Him for coming into the world for
you?*

Continue as above. Give each child a shoelace to keep,
if possible. Tell them that every time they tie their shoes
in the morning, they can remember that they are joined
together with Jesus. Each time the child ties a shoe, he/
she can remember and say, "Thank you, Jesus, that I'm
joined together with you."

Candlelight

Verse to memorize: "Again Jesus spoke to
them, saying, 'I am the light of the world; he
who follows me will not walk in darkness, but
will have the light of life'" (John 8:12).

*What am I holding in my hand? A candle,
yes. Why do we have candles? Right, to give
light. Is this candle giving off any light now?
No, because it isn't lit. If I were to light it,
would it give off light? Yes, it would. We have to
light the candle with fire so that it will give off*

193

light, as a candle is supposed to do.

In the Bible, Jesus calls Himself the "Light of the World," and the Bible also uses fire as one of the symbols of the Holy Spirit. Did you know that every person is like a candle? God created every person to receive Him. His desire is to come and be a part of every person's life, so that His light can be seen by others and so that His light can change our lives.

Is a candle made to give off light? Yes. (Light a match and light the candle.) Were we made by God for a purpose? Yes. We were made to have the light of Jesus Christ in us.

How do we receive Jesus Christ, the light, into our lives? Well, how does a candle receive light? First you decide to light the candle, then strike a match and set it on the wick. If I want to receive Jesus Christ into my life, I must ask Him to do so. Then His light can shine through me and His light can change me and make me to be the person He wants me to be.

I remember the time I asked Jesus to come into my life . . . . (Give a brief personal testimony.)

Would you like to have Jesus Christ come into your life and begin to change it so that you can be the person He wants you to be? He will come into your life if you want Him to and if you ask Him. Do you want to talk to Jesus right now and tell Him you want Him to come into your life?

Afterwards, give each of the children a candle to keep

and describe once more the symbol of Jesus as the light shining in them.

If you are a parent you can light the candle every night when praying together. A small candle may be set down into a large "pillar" candle to last indefinitely.

Jack-o'-Lantern

Similar to the candlelight approach, this method is especially useful at Halloween. As you are carving out the inside of a pumpkin, explain that just as there is a hollow place in the pumpkin, so there is a hollow place in every person's life who doesn't have Jesus Christ living within.

Carve out a smiley face on one side of the pumpkin. Explain that anyone can appear happy or can have a smiley face on the outside. But not everyone has the happiness of having Jesus Christ living in their lives. A pumpkin without a light in it isn't complete—it isn't doing what it was made to do. In the same way, a person without Jesus Christ isn't complete.

Explain that Jesus is called the "Light of the World" in the Bible. Explain that He can make a difference in our lives if we allow Him to come into us. Compare this to the difference that a light makes in the pumpkin. (Light a candle or turn on a flashlight and set it inside the pumpkin to illustrate.)

Continue as in the candle approach.

Use the pumpkin when sharing the child's decision with the family. Take a picture of the child with the jack-o'-lantern as a memory token.

Crackers

Can you bend this cracker without breaking it? And can you make this cracker become twice

*as large as it is now without breaking it? Both of
these are simple, but I'll need some water.*

Use a bowl of water at least twice the width of the
cracker. Set the cracker into the water, letting it float.
Occasionally submerge it so that the top becomes wet. In
a few moments the cracker will double in size and become
pliable so that it will fold in half without breaking.

*What do you think? Can I bend this cracker
without cracking it? Yes! Did I make this
cracker become twice as large without cracking
it? Yes! What was the secret? The water changed
the cracker, didn't it?*

*This little trick illustrates something about
ourselves. Sometimes we know what we ought to
do—like obey our parents or control our
tempers—but we just can't seem to do it. We are
like this cracker* (hold up a dry cracker). *We
need something to change our lives before we
can become the persons God wants us to be.*

*Do you remember the story in the Bible
about Jesus and the woman at the well of water?
Jesus says that He is living water that can
change our lives. Let's pretend that this water in
the bowl is Jesus Christ, okay? Let's pretend that
this cracker is you. Let's put you, the cracker,
into Jesus Christ, the water, and see again what
will happen.*

*Now look. The cracker is in the water,
right? And the water is also in the cracker,
right? Both are part of one another. That
cracker is changed because it is in the water.
The water is what changes it.*

If you are the cracker and the water is Jesus Christ, then you can be changed by Jesus Christ to do those things which you know you should do. Jesus, living in our hearts, makes all the difference in the world.

Do you want to let Jesus become part of your life, so that you can become everything He wants you to be? You can do that by talking with Jesus right now.

Continue as described above. A photograph of the child holding the crackers would be a nice memorial token.

The Door

Let's look at a verse in the Bible that talks about a door and Jesus Christ. It is found way in the back of the Bible in the book of Revelation:

Behold, I stand at the door and knock; if any one hears my voice ànd opens the door, I will come in (Rev. 3:20).

As I read the verse again, see if you can tell me what Jesus is doing. "Behold, I stand at the door and knock." What does that verse say that Jesus is doing? (Standing at the door.) *And what else is He doing?* (He's knocking. Read the verse again if necessary.)

Jesus is both standing at the door and He is knocking on the door, isn't He? Listen again and see if you can tell me what He is asking us to do: "Behold, I stand at the door and knock; if any one hears my voice and opens the door, I will come in."

Jesus is standing at the door and knocking.

197

What does He say that He wants us to do?
(Open the door.)

Listen again as I read the last part of the verse and tell me what Jesus will do if we open the door: "Behold, I stand at the door and knock; if any one hears my voice and opens the door, I will come in." (He will come in.)

That's right. Would you like to act out this verse together? Let me play the part of Jesus and you play the part of the person who hears Him knock.

At this point, the parent goes outside of the room and closes the door. Then knock on the door and call out the child's name and ask to come in. Have the child open the door and invite you to come into the room. Come in and get down to the child's level, giving a hug.

(Name of the child), thank you for inviting me to come in.

If desired, repeat the game, allowing the child to go outside the door and knock.

Let's talk about this. There are some people that we have seen on television, but we don't really know them as our own friends. They don't know our names or come to visit our family. Can you think of some people that you "know" on TV, but do not "know" as a friend? (If the child hesitates, make a few suggestions.)

Now, there are many people who know about Jesus. They know His name and they may know some things about Him, but not everyone knows Jesus as their personal friend. This verse tells us that Jesus wants to meet everyone and become their special friend. Jesus wants to become your personal friend, too. Jesus wants to share His love and care for you.

You know where your heart is, don't you? That's right, inside of you. We have feelings of love for one another in our hearts. Let's pretend that there is a door on your heart. Jesus is knocking on that door and calling you by name. He wants to come in and be your personal friend and share His love and happiness with you.

Would you like to invite Jesus to come into your heart and be your special friend? (If a child asks *how* Jesus can come inside of him/her, use ideas from the "spiritual breathing" approach.)

As a memory token, encourage the child to draw a picture of this image from Revelation 3:20. Tape the drawing to the door of the child's room. Put the date on the picture or perhaps set it in a simple frame to preserve it for the child.

The Gift

Although this illustration is most appropriate at Christmastime, at a birth or any celebration where gifts are exchanged, it may be adapted to other occasions. This presentation is made to a group of children. The visual aid is a box of candy with the top and bottom of the box wrapped separately so that the top will easily lift on and off without removing the ribbons and colored paper.

What do I have with me today? (A present.)
And who do you think this present is for? (Wait until someone says, "For us!") *For you?*

*Really? Well, you're right! Can you guess what
is inside?* (Solicit various ideas.) *Okay, would
somebody like to lift the lid carefully and take a
peek?* (Allow one child to do so.)

(Name), tell the children what is in the box
(candy)*! Would you like to have a piece? Okay,
take a piece, and eat it. Is it good? Tell the other
kids how good that candy is.* (Child tells the
children.)

*Now, do the rest of you want a piece of
candy?* (Yes, yes!) *Okay, (name), would you
pass around the box so that everyone may have a
piece of candy?*

*All right, was that a nice present? Yes, but
you didn't know what was in the box, until
(name) told you that it was candy. Then (name)
told you that it was good candy and you believed
(him/her). Suddenly you all wanted to have
what (name) had, right?*

*Well, God has given a present to each person
in the whole world and that present is Jesus
Christ, His Son.* (If it is Christmastime, briefly
mention that the birth of the Child was the first
Christmas present.)

*But lots of people don't know about God's
gift. Or perhaps they have heard some things
about Jesus, but they don't know how good it is
to have Him in their hearts. Maybe they don't
know that Jesus is God's gift for them,
personally.*

*So, just as (name) told you what was in the
box, people need to be told about Jesus. And just
as (name) told you that the candy is good, people
need to hear that Jesus is good. And one more*

thing. Just as you believed *(name) when (he/
she) told you the candy was good and you*
received *the candy from (him/her), people need
to* believe *in Jesus and* receive *Him into their
hearts.*

*When you believed (name), what was the
good thing you received?* (Candy.) *Can you tell
me some of the good things that happen in our
lives when we receive Jesus?* (No doubt they will
mention love, joy, eternal life, forgiveness,
etc. Affirm any and all answers.)

*The Bible says in John 1:12 that "to all who
received him, who believed in his name, he gave
power to become children of God." You can
receive God's gift, Jesus Christ, into your life
right now. You can talk to God, in prayer, and
tell Him that you* believe *that Jesus is His good
gift to you. You can also tell God that you want
to* receive *Jesus, now, in your heart. Would you
like to do that now?*

Continue as above. When working with a group, allow
those who are sure they already have Jesus in their hearts
to pray a prayer of thanksgiving for all He has already
given them. You can give each child a tiny ornamental "gift
box" such as a Christmas tree ornament as a memory
token.

Follow-up

When the one to lead a child to a personal commitment
to Christ is not a member of the immediate family, there
must be careful and deliberate follow-up. It is important
that during the first week after a child has made a prayer of

commitment, the helper visit the child, in his/her home if possible, to reinforce the new relationship with Jesus Christ. Telephone the parents before visiting.

After a brief get-acquainted time, the helper may refer to the memory token in some way. If you used the tied together illustration, look at the child's shoes (hopefully, they won't have Velcro!) and make a comment such as, "Oh, look at those shoelaces—they're tied! Do you remember what we did with the shoelace that I used this past week?" (Identify the place where the teaching occurred.) Other comments might include, "Have you been showing your friends the trick with the cracker?" or "I see a lovely candle on the table. Do you remember how we are like a candle?"

Affirm what the child did and that he/she is living in a new relationship with Jesus. The important thing is that repetition aids retention and lays a solid foundation upon which to build the many truths of the Scriptures. This foundation is necessary if the child is to expand on the knowledge of Jesus Christ.

The helper should covenant with God to pray regularly for each child that is led to Jesus Christ. A self-discipline of daily prayer for the child for 30 days seems appropriate in the beginning, followed by a commitment to pray regularly for the child through the years. Indeed, a lifetime prayer covenant is worth considering. God honors the prayers of intercession by His people!

Forgiveness

Parents and teachers often must deal with a child who has done something wrong, deliberately or accidentally. These unpleasant times are opportunities for communicating God's concern and forgiveness. The following approach may be used after a time of gentle correction and discipline.

(Name), what you did was wrong. All of us, including your mommy and daddy, your Sunday School teachers and pastors have done wrong things. We've done things like not always telling the truth, not always obeying our parents or our boss, maybe fighting with others, thinking mean thoughts about others or calling others bad names.

The Bible's word for doing these wrong things is "sin." The Bible also says that because we have done these wrong things and sinned, we deserve to be punished. We feel terrible when we know we've done wrong. How do you feel when you've done something wrong? (You may hear "terrible," "dirty," "sick at my tummy," "I hate myself." Sometimes a "tough guy" will say, "I feel fine!" If so, just continue, saying, *"Most of us feel bad inside"* because of course the child really *does* feel bad and knows it.)

Because God loves us, He sent His Son, Jesus, to come to each of us and to forgive us for all the wrong things that we have done. He wants to love us and make us feel good inside. He also wants us to know that we are forgiven for the wrongs that we have done—just like it feels good for me to give you a hug and say that I forgive you for the wrong thing that you did. Jesus wants you to know that you are forgiven.

Would you like to talk to Jesus right now and ask Him to forgive you of all the wrong things that you have done? You can tell Him just how you feel inside and ask Him to make

203

you feel good and (clean, well, lovely) again. If
you like, I will talk to Him first, because He is
my friend, too, and has forgiven me for wrong
things that I have done. Then you can talk to
Him in your own words.

Briefly thank Jesus for this special moment and this special child. Ask Jesus to be real to the child as you pray together. Allow the child to pray, then spend some time asking the child if he/she has any "different" feelings. Help the child understand that Jesus has indeed forgiven him/her, whether there are different feelings or not. It is like when we remove a bandage sometimes the spot stings a little, even after the bandage is gone. If the child is old enough, read and memorize 1 John 1:9.

There are times when a child who has a personal relationship with Jesus becomes distressed with his/her own behavior. I have found this to be a common problem as children approach puberty and become more aware of their own faults and failures. The child may believe that if Jesus resided in the heart, there would be no more bad thoughts or disobedience—ever! When this is the case, the child may become very angry at herself, feel that she is "losing Jesus" or that God doesn't love her anymore.

The parent or teacher should encourage the child to talk about these feelings and about any fears or confusion he/she may have. Then remind the child that Jesus taught us to call God "our Father":

Do you remember when you were learning to
walk? You can't because you were too little. But
just for a minute, think about a little baby (boy/
girl) whose daddy is teaching (him/her) how to

walk. The daddy takes the baby by the hand and supports the baby as those first few steps are taken. Now, tell me, is it the baby's grip on the daddy's finger that holds the baby up or is it the daddy's strong grip that supports the baby? That's right, it's the daddy's grip. In just the same way, God the Father supports us. He knows that we are not strong enough to do everything we are supposed to do or to be perfect all the time, so He holds us up Himself.

Now, think about the baby again. Sometime the daddy will let go of the baby's hand and let the baby take a few steps alone. What happens? That's right, the baby falls down. Maybe the baby even gets hurt and doesn't want to try again. Now, what does the daddy say? Does he get angry and yell at the baby, saying, "Bad baby! I told you not to fall down!" No, of course not. Daddy helps the baby up, gives some more support for awhile, then encourages the baby to go it alone again.

That's just the way God is. He doesn't want us to fall down and hurt ourselves. The bad things we do, our sins, can hurt us and hurt other people. That is why God teaches us about sin and shows us the right things to do. But when we fail, fall down and hurt ourselves, He is right here to forgive us and help us to feel better and to get us doing the right thing again.

Would you like to pray together, asking God to forgive your sin and to assure you of His forgiveness and love? Would you like for me to pray first? Then you can pray in your own words.

Proceed accordingly. After praying, read together 1 John 1:9 and repeat the following assurance: *God has forgiven (child's name) sins and cleansed (name) from all unrighteousness.*

It's Good News

Tell your children of it, and let your children tell their children, and their children another generation (Joel 1:3).

This verse from Joel refers to a great drought that struck Israel and it makes me wonder: if the bad news was so important to communicate to future generations, what about the Good News? Fathers, let's give ourselves to the high calling of telling our children about Jesus Christ, for if we have taught them how to pass on the Good News, their own children will tell yet another generation.

Appendix

How to Get Started

Although there is certainly value in learning the principles of the FATHERS Ministry, the true purpose of this book is to encourage men to join together in fellowship and support groups, to learn together and to encourage one another. There are already growing numbers of FATHERS Ministries in cities across the United States and overseas and it is my vision that these groups are but the seeds of a growing awareness among Christian men in this generation.

Therefore this appendix is included to provide specific steps to equip you to initiate a FATHERS Ministry in your own community.

Work Through Channels

After initial personal prayer for God's leading and empowering in your intentions, approach your pastor and/or ruling body in your church. Describe your vision, sharing this book and the basic ideas of the FATHERS Ministry. Explain that you intend to proceed within the authority of the church, but that you expect that the fellowship will be totally self-regulating and self-supported. Explore the possibilities of using the church facilities, pending the desires of the members of the group.

Sound the Call

Pastors: Initiate the call through a sermon on the biblical teachings for Christian husbands and fathers, building on the examples of successes and failures in both the Old and New Testaments. You might want to work through a series on the family or focus on one "Father's Day" sermon. But each message should conclude with a call for men to make a specific response, indicating your vision for a continuing FATHERS Ministry.

Laymen: Many churches provide some format through which laypersons may make announcements or short presentations within the Sunday morning worship service. The Presbyterians often allow for a "Minute for Missions." Within 60 seconds it should be possible to:

1. Describe the need: "We need to learn *how* to become good husbands and fathers." (Refer to Ephesians 5:25 and 6:4.)
2. Suggest the program: "If you are interested in meeting weekly with a group of Christian men to hold one another accountable and learn to discipline ourselves to be the fathers that God would have us be . . . . "
3. Clearly state how they may respond and set a limited time for response: "Write a short note to me within the next three weeks, expressing your desire, and I will contact you regarding the time and place of our organizational meeting . . . . "

This same information should be printed in the Sunday morning bulletin, preferably for two or three consecutive weeks, as well as in the church newsletter.

In addition to Sunday morning announcements and notices in the bulletin and newsletter, prepare a direct mailing for key men in the congregation whom you would like God to bring into FATHERS. Pray for these men specifically, that they will be guided by the Holy Spirit. Write a personal letter modeled after my letter included in chapter one. Send it to *more* men than you actually expect will respond.

First Meeting

When the response time has passed, review the responses. If there are more responses than expected, pray for guidance whether to include all in the first meeting or to invite only 12 or so chosen men. If you chose *not* to include all the respondents, indicate this decision with a letter such as:

> Dear Prospective Fathers:
> This letter is to acknowledge that I have received your letter of application for the FATHERS Ministry. I am in the process of praying and seeking to *listen* to God, rather than to *talk* to Him, since I feel that He is the One who has led me in this direction through His voice to my own heart and mind. As soon as the application period is over (date), I will be informing you of the Lord's leading. Thank you for your prayers concerning this ministry.

Set a time at your own convenience and notify the

respondents. Repeat your intention that this fellowship is forming for the purpose of *discipline* and *accountability*. On the following page is a model letter I have used.

During the first meeting, you will:

a. Establish a meeting time, preferably an early weekday morning.

b. Establish a meeting place, convenient to all.

c. Introduce yourselves to one another by starting off with, "One thing about myself that I would like for you to remember is . . . . "

d. Pass out copies of the FATHERS' Oath and the FATHERS' Covenant and discuss.

e. Consider possible books to study together, specifically this text as well as the Bible study guide, *This Morning with God* or something similar. Other titles are listed in the bibliography.

f. Choose a format or "theme" for the group.

g. State that at the next meeting the company will be divided into squads, naming a squad leader who will serve during the next few months. Each FATHERS member will be paired with a buddy.

h. Take a photograph of each FATHERS member to mount on a bulletin board. Ask fathers to bring photos of wives and children to share with each other.

i. Collect information for I.D.s (dog tags), including names of wife and children.

Themes

Military Theme

At College Hill we began by using a military format, which has worked well for us. Other groups have found that some members respond negatively to a military format.

Dear Father:

Please join us at (place, date, hour) for the planning and organizational meeting of

> **F**athers
> **A**ccountable
> **T**o
> **H**ealthy
> **E**nduring
> **R**elationships and
> **S**pirituality.

It has been a special privilege to be thinking and praying this past (month) about our future ministry together. I have been led to extend an invitation to (all/only a few) of those who have given serious thought and prayer to this ministry. Those who come will understand that we each expect to commit ourselves to this ministry for at least two years. We will meet this first time to become acquainted with one another and to set up our future meeting times. I am anticipating an early morning type of meeting at some place central to all of us, so as not to interfere with our times with families in the evening.

I am looking forward to being with you.

In the Grace of God,

- Leaders: Company Commander, Sergeant, Officers, Squads and Squad leaders
- Weekly assignments: marching orders
- Bible: sword or "weapon"
- FATHERS members lift Bibles for reciting oath: "Present arms!"
- Buddies exchange "dog tags" with personal information: name, address and phone number, spouse's name, children's names and ages.
- FATHERS members missing meeting: AWOL/AWL. Keep a squad card.
- Closing prayer: commissioning.

Sports Theme

I believe this is a good theme with lots of creative potential (without the possible negative implications of the military format). Also, the weekly "score card" implies a less-demanding standard than the military "squad card."

- Leaders: Team Captains, Coaches, Managers.
- Squad leaders: Quarterbacks, Assistant Coaches.
- Weekly assignments: game plans.
- With or without Bible: "in-" or "out-of-uniform."

Initial Instructions to Recruits/Rookies

1. Place Bibles on the family table during meals. Use at least one verse to preface all prayers of thanksgiving for the food.

2. Affirm your wife daily (at supper) by stating at least three positive characteristics about her.

3. Pray daily for your buddy and for the FATHERS Ministry.

4. Always carry your sword/equipment (Bible).
5. Begin to memorize our Oath, word perfect!

The FATHERS Covenant

This book (covenant) of the law shall not depart out of your mouth, but you shall meditate on it day and night, that you may be careful to do according to all that is written in it; for then you shall make your way *prosperous,* and then you shall have good success (Joshua 1:8, italics added).

On my honor, I covenant to do my best to do all that is written in this covenant in order that my way shall be PROSPEROUS:

P - *Pray* regularly for the fathers and the FATHERS Ministry. (See Phil. 1:3-6.)

R - *Regularly* attend the meetings unless prohibited by unavoidable conflicts. When such occasions occur, I will notify the appropriate leadership. (See Heb. 10:24-25.)

O - *Only* give a good report about other fathers and the FATHERS Ministry. (See Eph. 4:29.)

S - *Safeguard* the confidentiality of other FATHERS members. (See Prov. 18:8-21.)

P - *Preserve* time for the Lord in my daily schedule. (See Matt. 6:6.)

E - *Exemplify* the life of Christ in my life. (See Col. 2:6-7.)

R - *Regularly* worship with the Body of Christ. (See Acts 2:6-7.)

213

O - *Observe* a weekly clubtime with my wife and each child. (See Phil. 2:4.)
U - *Uphold* the daily themes:
    M - Mother's day
    T - Take Time
    W - Worship
    Th - Thanksgiving
    F - Family
    S - Sexuality
    S - Schedule Sharing.
S - *Serve* my family members and others. (See Mark 10:45.)

Meeting Format

1. Opening oath led by volunteer. To "present arms" stand at attention, hold Bible in right hand and extended in salute.
2. Opening prayer led by volunteer.
3. Confession and forgiveness of latecomers.
4. Announcements of those AWOL.
5. Company concerns.
6. Teaching time. Initial teachings may cover the basics of this book:
    a. Time with the Father of fathers
    b. Time with your wife
    c. Clubtime with each child
    d. Scheduling, etc.
    e. Other teachings that this text has not covered but which FATHERS have studied include family budgeting, sibling rivalry, sick and aging parents/grandparents, job changes, career choices, buying/renting homes, coping with depression, dealing with death,

questions of divorce and remarriage, single parenting, etc.

7. Squad Time:
    a. Log-in time. How are you doing? Discuss specific victories, failures, needs, joys, personal concerns, etc.
    b. Check buddies' score cards/squad cards.
    c. Personal prayer.
8. Weekly assignment.
9. Commissioning.

Long-term Planning

After six months, set a special meeting for review and evaluation. Invite wives to write a note indicating their observations, approval or criticisms. Determine where the ministry is achieving its goals and where more discipline is needed.

Plan some fun times:
- Christmas party with wives and kids.
- Sweetheart Ball in February (without kids) that includes flowers for wives, fancy attire, dinner or snacks.
- Memorial Day picnic to set up the Memorial Stone (see chapter 8).
- Harvest Potluck.

Plan some special times:
- Design and construct a "Memorial" of some type.
- Set a date for FATHERS members to solemnly sign the Covenant.
- Arrange for FATHERS members and their wives to

215

take the Myers-Briggs Personal Preference Profile
or a similar evaluation.
- Read and discuss *Please Understand Me.*

Continue to evaluate the ministry every six months.
At the end of two years, chose mature FATHERS members
to become leaders of the next "generation." Send out the
call for new recruits/rookies.

Notes

Chapter 1

1. James Dobson, *Straight Talk to Men and Their Wives* (Waco, TX: Word Books, 1980), pp. 130-133.
2. Dr. Urie Bronfenbrenner, "Origins of Alienation," *Scientific American* (August, 1974), p. 54.
3. For the purpose of reading ease, the name of the organization will be referred to as FATHERS throughout the rest of this book.

Chapter 2

1. Carol Adeney, ed., *This Morning with God* (Downers Grove, IL: InterVarsity Press, 1978).
2. David Keirsey and Marilyn Bates, *Please Understand Me: Character and Temperament Types* (Del Mar, CA: Prometheus Nemesis Book Co., Inc., 1978).
3. For further reading on personality preference types, see:
   Isabel Briggs Myers with Peter B. Myers, *Gifts Differing* (Palo Alto, CA: Consulting Psychologists Press, Inc., 1980).
   Chester P. Michael and Marie C. Norrisey, *Prayer and Temperament* (Charlottesville, VA: The Open Door Inc., 1984).
4. See 2 Timothy 2:15.
5. See Ephesians 5:25.
6. See Ephesians 6:4.
7. See Deuteronomy 6:6-7.
8. See Joshua 24:15.
9. See Philippians 4:13.
10. Squad meetings occur during every FATHERS meeting and make up the heart of the ministry. The small squads (usually combining four fathers—two under 35 and two over 35) move to various available corners in the meeting room and discuss, in a heart-to-heart way, the lesson that was presented that evening. The amazing ability of the men to care for each other, bear

each other's burdens and share those things of the heart has inspired the ministry beyond any other activity. The men spend at least six months in a squad and the opportunity for the participants to sound off each other, make themselves vulnerable to each other and learn from each other makes it often very difficult to rearrange the squads. Prayer, weekly contact and consistent friendships are important aspects of the squad meetings.

Chapter 3
1. Joseph Procaccini and Mark W. Kiefaber, *Parent Burnout* (New York: Doubleday & Co., Inc., 1983).
2. *Ibid.*

Chapter 4
1. James Dobson, *What Wives Wish Their Husbands Knew About Women* (Wheaton, IL: Tyndale House Publishers, 1975).

Chapter 5
1. James Dobson, *What Wives Wish Their Husbands Knew About Women* (Wheaton, IL: Tyndale House Publishers, 1975), p. 164.

Chapter 6
1. Willis Barnstone, ed., *The Other Bible* (San Francisco: Harper and Row, 1984), p. 306.
2. I recommend two good programs to aid in Scripture memorization:
   The Navigators Topical Memory System
   P.O. Box 6000
   Colorado Springs, CO 80934
   Wise Words for Boys and Girls
   Bible Memory Association International
   P.O. Box 12000
   St. Louis, MO 63112
3. Jean Fleming, *A Mother's Heart* (Colorado Springs: Navpress, 1982), p. 87.

Chapter 8
1. Edith Schaeffer, *What Is a Family?* (Old Tappan, NJ: Fleming H. Revell, 1975), p. 189.
2. *Ibid.*, p. 199.

Chapter 10
1. James Dobson, *Straight Talk to Men and Their Wives* (Waco, TX: Word Books, 1980), p. 52.

Bibliography

Adeney, Carol, ed. *This Morning with God*. Downers Grove, IL: InterVarsity Press, 1978.

Arthur, Kay. *Lord, I Want to Know You*. Old Tappan, NJ: Fleming H. Revell, 1984.

Blitchington, W. Peter. *Sex Roles and the Christian Family*. Wheaton, IL: Tyndale House Publishers, 1984.

Brenneman, Helen Good. *Meditations for the Expectant Mother*. Scottsdale, PA: Herald Press, 1968.

Briggs, Dorothy Corkille. *Your Child's Self-Esteem*. New York: Doubleday & Co., Inc., 1975.

Campbell, Ross. *How to Really Love Your Child*. Wheaton, IL: Victor Books.

Chambers, Oswald. *Daily Thoughts for Disciples*. Grand Rapids, MI: Zondervan Publishing House, 1976.

Chapin, Alice. *Building Your Child's Faith*. San Bernardino, CA: Here's Life Publishers, 1983.

Coleman, William. *Before You Tuck Me In*. Minneapolis: Bethany House Publishers, 1985.

———. *The Good Night Book*. Minneapolis: Bethany House Publishers, 1979.

———. *The Warm Hug Book*. Minneapolis: Bethany House Publishers, 1985.

Curran, Dolores. *Traits of a Healthy Family*. Minneapolis: Winston Press, 1983.

Dobson, James. *Dare to Discipline.* Wheaton, IL: Tyndale House Publishers, 1973.

———. *Dr. Dobson Answers Your Questions.* Wheaton, IL: Tyndale House Publishers, 1982.

———. *Hide or Seek.* Old Tappan, NJ: Fleming H. Revell, 1974.

———. *Love Must Be Tough.* Waco, TX: Word Books, 1983.

———. *Preparing for Adolescence.* Ventura, CA: Regal Books, 1978.

———. *Straight Talk to Men and Their Wives.* Waco, TX: Word Books, 1980.

———. *The Strong-Willed Child.* Wheaton, IL: Tyndale House Publishers, 1978.

———. *What Wives Wish Their Husbands Knew About Women.* Wheaton, IL: Tyndale House Publishers, 1975.

Dodson, Fitzhugh. *How to Father.* New York: New American Library, 1975.

Durka, Gloria and Smith, Joanmarie, eds. *Family Ministry.* Minneapolis: Winston Press, 1980.

Encyclopedia of Christian Marriage. Old Tappan, NJ: Fleming H. Revell, 1982.

Encyclopedia of Christian Marriage. Old Tappan, NJ: Fleming H. Revell, 1984.

Friedman, Edwin H. *Generation to Generation.* New York: The Guilford Press, 1985.

Ginott, Dr. Haim G. *Between Parent and Child.* New York: Avon Books, 1956.

Joy, Donald M. *Bonding: Relationship in the Image of God.* Waco, TX: Word Books, 1985.

Keirsey, David and Bates, Marilyn. *Please Understand Me.* Del Mar, CA: Prometheus Nemesis Book Co., Inc., 1984.

Kesler, Jay. *Parents and Teenagers.* Wheaton, IL: Victor Books, 1984.

Klaus, Marshall H. *Parent-Infant Bonding.* St. Louis: C. V. Mosby Co., 1982.

Kramer, Rita. *In Defense of the Family.* New York: Basic Books, Inc. 1983.

Lee, R. S. *Your Growing Child and Religion.* New York: Macmillan Publishing Co., Inc., 1963.

Leman, Kevin. *The Birth Order Book.* Old Tappan, NJ: Fleming H. Revell, 1984.

MacDonald, Gordon. *Magnificent Marriage.* Wheaton, IL: Tyndale House Publishers, 1984.

Mayhall, Jack and Carole. *Marriage Takes More Than Love.* Colorado Springs: Navpress, 1978.

Meier, Paul D. *Christian Child-Rearing and Personality Development.* Grand Rapids, MI: Baker Book House, 1977.

Meier, Paul and Meier, Richard. *Family Foundations.* Grand Rapids, MI: Baker Book House, 1981.

Meier, Richard, et al. *Sex in the Christian Marriage.* Richardson, TX: Today Pub., Inc., 1985.

Michael, Chester and Norrisey, Marie. *Prayer and Temperament: Different Prayer Forms for Different Personality Types.* Charlottesville, VA: The Open Door, Inc., 1984.

Myers, Isabel Briggs with Myers, Peter B. *Gifts Differing.* Palo Alto, CA: Consulting Psychologists Pr., Inc., 1980.

Narramore, Bruce. *Help! I'm a Parent.* Grand Rapids, MI: Zondervan Publishing House, 1972.

Penner, Clifford and Joyce. *The Gift of Sex.* Waco, TX: Word Books, 1981.

Procaccini, Joseph with Kiefaber, Mark. *Parent Burnout.* New York: Doubleday & Co., Inc., 1983.

Rekers, Dr. George. *Family Building.* Ventura, CA: Regal Books, 1985.

————. *Shaping Your Child's Sexual Identity.* Grand Rapids, MI: Baker Book House, 1982.

Sanford, John and Paula. *The Elijah Task.* Tulsa, OK: Victory House, 1986.

————. *Restoring the Christian Family.* Plainfield, NJ: Logos International, 1979.

Schaeffer, Edith. *What Is a Family?* Old Tappan, NJ: Fleming H. Revell, 1975.

Shelly, Judith Allen. *The Spiritual Needs of Children.* Downers Grove, IL: InterVarsity Press, 1982.

Sherrill, Helen Hardwicke. *Christian Parenthood.* Richmond, VA: CLC Press, 1964.

Smedes, Lewis B. *Forgive and Forget.* New York: Pocket Books, Inc., 1984.

Swindoll, Charles R. *Strike the Original Match.* Portland, OR: Multnomah Press, 1980.

Tengborn, Mildred. *Devotions for a New Mother.* Minneapolis, MN: Bethany House Publishers, 1977.

Wheat, Ed and Wheat, Gaye. *Intended for Pleasure.* Old Tappan, NJ: Fleming H. Revell, 1977.

Wheat, Ed. *Love Life.* Grand Rapids, MI: Zondervan Publishing House, 1980.

Williams, H. Page. *Do Yourself a Favor: Love Your Wife.* Plainfield, NJ: Logos International, 1973.

Wilson, Earl D. *Loving Enough to Care.* Portland, OR: Multnomah Press, 1984.

Wright, H. Norman. *Communication: Key to Your Marriage.* Ventura, CA: Regal Books, 1974.

————. *More Communication Keys for Your Marriage.* Ventura, CA: Regal Books, 1983.

————. *Seasons of a Marriage.* Ventura, CA: Regal Books, 1982.